ISSUE LEADERSHIP

ISSUE LEADERSHIP

A Guide for Those That
Want to Make a Positive Change
in the World

KEVAN & ALEXA LAMM

Copyright © 2019 — Kevan & Alexa Lamm

ALL RIGHTS RESERVED—No part of this book may be reproduced in any form or by any electronic or mechanical means, including information storage and retrieval systems, without permission in writing from the author, except by a reviewer who may quote brief passages in a review.

Published by Deeds Publishing in Athens, GA
www.deedspublishing.com

Printed in The United States of America

Cover design by Mark Babcock. Text layout by Matt King.

ISBN 978-1-947309-80-7

Books are available in quantity for promotional or premium use. For information, email info@deedspublishing.com.

First Edition, 2019

10 9 8 7 6 5 4 3 2 1

For Charlotte, Warren, and Aiden — this is our attempt to make the world you will inherit a better place. We love you and are infinitely proud of you.

— Mom & Dad

CONTENTS

Introduction   1

Background   9
   The Leadership Journey   13

The Framework   19
   Action   21
      Advocacy   22
      Assume Leadership Roles and Increase Involvement   24
      Mentor   26
      Network   27
      Expand Issue Engagement   35
      Serve as a Resource   40
      Summary   42
   Change   45
      Act as a Change Agent   47
      Innovation   49
      Risk-Taking   53
      Self-Efficacy   56
      Summary   58
   Communication   61
      Listening   62
      Persuasive Speaking   66
      Written and Oral Communications   69
      Media Relations   72
      Summary   75
   Relationships & Character   79
      Confidence   80

Empathy	*84*
Ethics	*88*
Initiative	*91*
Integrity	*94*
Life-Long Learning	*97*
Motivation	*101*
Self-Awareness	*107*
Understanding and Appreciating Diversity	*111*
Summary	*115*
Strategic Planning	117
Critical Thinking	*119*
Decision Making	*123*
Global and Systems Thinking	*126*
Goal Setting and Visioning	*130*
Problem Solving	*134*
Stakeholder Assessment	*139*
Summary	*144*
Supporting	147
Conflict Management	*148*
Fostering and Enabling Others	*154*
Issue Awareness	*158*
Political Process Awareness	*163*
Recognizing Values	*167*
Summary	*171*
Coordinating	173
CollaBoration	*175*
Group and Team Dynamics	*179*
Policy Influence	*184*

Trust Building	*187*
Summary	*192*

Putting It All Together 195
Issue Leadership	*200*
Next Steps	*200*

Acknowledgements 203

About the Authors 205

INTRODUCTION

On Friday, July 26, 2013, our 19-week-old daughter underwent open heart surgery.

It felt like my wife and I were the ones on the operating table. Like we were having our hearts ripped from our chests. We had been trying to start a family for years before our beautiful, perfect little girl was born, and now—and now—

Sometimes in life, there are moments of absolute clarity. This was one of them. The trappings of success, which had driven us for decades, fell away. What was the good of new cars and bigger houses if our daughter died?

Family, love, purpose, and meaning. That Friday was the major turning point of our lives, but it didn't come out of nowhere. Our journey had started many years before; we just hadn't realized it.

My wife and I were both blessed to grow up in loving homes with amazing and caring parents. Although we lived in different parts of the country, we were both drawn to agriculture and horseback riding. These were our earliest classrooms, where we learned life lessons in commitment, hard work, and self-reliance. We were both very involved in sports and the 4-H youth development program. In fact, it was Alexa's swimming that brought her to Colorado State University, where we met.

As is the case with most young love, we had our challenges; however, we surpassed them. We graduated—Alexa with a Master's in Education and me, Kevan, with a bachelor's degree in Mechanical Engineering—and got married shortly after.

That was around the turn of the millennium, which was an interesting time to begin a new career. I immediately began working for Accenture, a consulting and professional services firm, and Alexa began working as a 4-H agent in the Denver metro area. Our backgrounds and upbringings drove us to be outwardly successful. New cars, a new house, and 80-hour weeks working towards promotions and awards—these were the things we thought were important.

At the beginning of our careers, the "fake it until you make it," "anything goes," and "take what you want" mentalities ruled the business world. Tech seemed poised for an endless boom, IPOs were the quickest way to riches, and anything was possible. That was also when *Survivor*, the CBS juggernaut, was introduced to American audiences. Millions of us watched Richard Hatch manipulate his way to the first $1 million grand prize.

It was a renaissance of the "all about me" 80s. If you wanted something, you took it. Need someone to look up to? Try the titans of industry: Ken Lay, Dennis Kozlowski, or Bernie Ebbers. If you were willing to do what it took, the possibilities were limitless.

And then it all came crashing down. Billions and billions in market value vanished, and many of us in tech space suddenly began wondering how we were going to pay for the lifestyles we were indebted to. The downfall of Enron hit me particularly close to home. When I joined Accenture, it was known as Andersen Consulting. That's right: it was the consulting arm of the now-infamous Arthur Andersen accounting firm.

I went through my initial training with Accenture right after the arbitration between Andersen Consulting and Arthur Andersen.

That was an interesting time, because the onsite training facility in St. Charles, IL housed individuals from both organizations. Individuals who'd previously been colleagues were now potential competitors!

Following Enron's bankruptcy in December of 2001, what we'd originally considered a blow showed itself to be a gift. As Enron's accounting firm, Arthur Andersen (and the Andersen name) was pulled under. The newly rebranded Accenture was generally unblemished in the debacle, although it was difficult not to think about the individuals who had recently been at St. Charles and who, through no fault of their own, were now unemployed.

Once the dot-com bubble burst and major players such as Tyco and WorldCom went under, it was almost certain that the consulting industry would take a significant hit; it did. One of the worst places to be was on the bench, which is the time between client projects. Unfortunately, I was benched during this tumultuous period.

To fill the time of unstaffed employees, a week-long training was scheduled. At the beginning of the week, almost 50 of us crammed into a conference room to learn about web programming. The first two days were great, a nice distraction, but reality hit us on Wednesday.

Starting at about 10 a.m., members of my class began receiving phone calls asking them to go up to the partner's floor for meetings. It started slowly: two or three individuals in the first hour, with more and more getting calls as the morning dragged on. At first, it was not clear what the meetings were about. Perhaps a new project and staffing opportunities?

No. When individuals left to attend their meetings, they did not return. These were not staffing meetings; they were termination meetings.

The mood in the room shifted from anxiety to panic. Any of us might be next. If we were, this would be our last day.

At the end of the week, only 12 of us were left. I was one of the 12, and I'll never forget that time. It wasn't just my office, either; this was happening in offices all over Denver, all over the United States, and all over the world. Leaders had chosen recklessly, and other people were paying for their mistakes.

However—and this is important—even during this difficult time, human character and resiliency shone through. People found opportunities and kept moving forward. The sun continued to rise.

Although the following weeks were tense for those of us on the bench, eventually new opportunities presented themselves. For me, this meant working in a new training center and traveling to India to start a new office location. That's something I might never have done otherwise. Going to India felt like traveling to the moon for someone who'd grown up in northern Colorado!

India was also a reality check. I'll never think about poverty the same way again; not now that I've witnessed children, dogs, and cows sifting through the same garbage to find food. I'll never think about opportunity and drive the same way; not once I realized that the man wearing a perfectly pressed security suit who was posted at the building I worked in 12 hours a day lived with his wife and three kids in a 12-foot by 12-foot plywood home with a tin roof and a tarp to keep out the rain.

Once I opened up to the possibility, I could not escape an ethos of change, community, and opportunity.

Life looked very different to me when I returned stateside. That Lexus in the driveway had lost some of the shine. The cable package with all possible premium channels seemed less fulfilling.

As I was having these revelations, Alexa began discovering the joys and struggles of working with youth. She saw and experienced the best and worst in people. She watched a 16-year-old teach a 10-year-old how to feed a horse, and her heart burst with pride. She endured an outraged parent spitting in her face when their child didn't win at the County Fair. Like me, she was learning perspective—on victory and on life.

ISSUE LEADERSHIP

After almost a decade of working with youth, Alexa knew it was time to pursue her lifelong dream of a doctoral degree. We moved to Florida to accommodate her. The move was right during the early stages of the housing meltdown, a second economic calamity in less than a decade.

The lessons from the dot-com bubble had not only been ignored; they'd been doubled down on. Again, innocent people suffered due to self-centered, callous leaders and other individuals.

And again, people did not learn. Instead of treating the housing mess as the consequence of greed and hubris, people acted as if it were an act of God, a force that was both unknowable and unstoppable! Plenty of people cast blame at bankers, mortgage brokers, and the 1%, but how many took personal responsibility? Who had the fortitude to say, "I not only recognize these issues, I want to do something about them"?

It was a pivotal time for us and for the nation. We needed to make a change.

After graduating with her Ph.D., Alexa was offered an amazing opportunity to stay with the University of Florida and be the director of the National Public Policy Evaluation Center. Once again, we'd "made it." I had a very successful career with one of the world's top consulting firms, and Alexa had a faculty position at a prestigious university. We tried to embrace our stability, but something wasn't right. Something was missing.

After hours, days, weeks, and months of discussion, prayer, and reflection, we decided that the best thing we could do was shake things up. At first, the destination for our journey was unclear, but we knew we needed to do something, and it had to be something big. We couldn't sit on the sidelines and watch the next housing bubble burst or stock market crash knowing we could have prevented it.

It was our duty to do what we could do to make the world a better place.

Although Accenture was an amazing place to work, and I had met some of the smartest and most talented individuals anywhere, it was time for me to say goodbye. This was a particularly difficult decision, because we were expecting our first child and the idea of giving up a six-figure salary to become a graduate student seemed foolish. Nevertheless, we knew what we were being called to do.

My first year in graduate school at the University of Florida was humbling, to say the least. After over a decade of being a manager, having multi-million dollar budgets, and conducting high level client meetings, I was cramming for quizzes and writing book reports. More than once, we questioned whether I was doing the right thing and if I should try to get my old job back.

In March, our daughter was born. Three days later, the pediatrician listened to her heart, and the smile dropped from her face. She immediately sent us to the pediatric cardiology unit of our local hospital for further tests.

Our daughter had a serious heart murmur. She needed open-heart surgery.

Shaking and terrified, my wife and I agreed to schedule the surgery. It would take place in July. Our daughter would be just four months old.

Sleepless nights, classwork, and studying are an exhausting cocktail. When that fateful day in July arrived, I was a total mess. I also wasn't prepared. Neither of us was. It's not possible to be prepared, not for something like this. Yes, we had met the surgical team and knew it was one of the best in the world. But that wasn't enough. We were handing over our beautiful baby girl, the thing we loved and cherished most in the universe, and we knew we might never get her back. We might never get to hold her again. Never to see her walk, graduate high school, get married. Never see any of thing things we imagined for her.

We said goodbye, knowing she might die.

The doctors took our baby girl away, and we returned to our car and cried. Not just cried—sobbed. Ugly, wailing cries for a solid 10 minutes. Then we collected ourselves, hugged, prayed, and went back inside to wait.

And wait.

Hours later, the surgeon returned and told us the news. The surgery had been a success. Although she would have a long recovery, our daughter could have a full life ahead of her.

We would see her grow up.

That was our turning point—those days leading up to and immediately following the surgery. Those were the days of clarity and purpose, and this is what my wife and I realized:

> *Everything in this life is about people. People who do heart surgery on newborns, grow crops, volunteer, whatever. Whoever you are and whatever you do, you have a purpose. Everyone has a purpose. Everyone has something to contribute. Everyone has a part to play in solving the issues we face in our world.*

As our daughter recovered, my wife and I resumed life with greater direction. We now knew what our purpose was: to help people better understand what it takes to make a difference—and, specifically, how to be an exceptional leader.

Issue Leadership had been born.

Issue Leadership is not a managerial theory intended to improve quarterly performance, although it might. It is the perspective that the world has limitless opportunities for people to do good, both professionally and personally. Everyone can and should be a leader; and through exceptional leadership, we can make a better world.

For six years, this has been our mission. We've read, researched, interviewed experts, and reflected on our personal experiences, both the good and the bad. We've studied the human dimensions of leadership through over $40 million in grant funding, and we've traveled the world from Kansas City, Missouri, to Ica, Peru, to Kampala, Uganda and Townsville, Australia. We've learned all we could from as many great leaders as we could find.

The result is this book.

Thank you for joining us on our mission to make this world a better place — a place where all our sons and daughters can grow up and make their own contributions. Together, we can make an amazing future.

Kevan and Alexa Lamm, 2019

BACKGROUND

Leadership is a process whereby an individual influences a group of individuals to achieve a common goal.

—*Peter Northouse*

Congratulations on taking the next step to becoming an exceptional leader! Being a leader is not necessarily about being a manager, holding a specific position, or having power over others. Being a leader is about influence, and that influence can come from anywhere.

Leadership as a concept has been studied extensively throughout history. From Sun Tzu's *The Art of War* and India's *Bhagavad Gita*, written in the sixth century BC, to Plato, Machiavelli, Shakespeare, Tolstoy, and Freud, to the people of today—leadership permeates all cultures around the globe. In academic literature, over 135 unique models of leadership have been proposed using over 1,000 different leadership factors. It's no wonder there's so much confusion on the subject!

Are leaders born or made? That's one of the first questions to arise in any discussion of leadership. All of us have some idea of what a leader is supposed to look like. Perhaps we visualize a political or religious leader or someone of a certain gender, of a certain age, and with a certain set of physical characteristics—perhaps tall, dark, and handsome? The reality is that leaders come in all shapes and sizes. They are of all genders and ages, and they have as many different physical characteristics as you can imagine. Time and again, research has shown that anyone, anywhere, at any time can become a leader.

Leadership is an exciting opportunity, but it can be overwhelming. Some people feel like it's impossible for them to become a leader, which is a totally normal reaction. Much like anything in life, the key to finishing a journey is starting.

With the right tools, attitude, and intention, you can become an exceptional leader!

The first key to successful leadership development is having the right mindset. Leadership is mostly about acquired ability, not talent. Think about a professional basketball player. Someone who is well over six feet tall might have an immediate physical advantage, but if that individual never puts forth the necessary effort to develop their basketball skills, they will never be a good player. Talent does not guarantee success; nor does lacking of physical qualities prevent someone from becoming an outstanding basketball player. For example, Spud Webb spent 13 years in the NBA confounding much taller opponents with his work ethic and attitude. He was only a little over five-and-a-half feet tall!

There are things that come easy to each of us, and there are things that we have to work hard to obtain. The key mindset to success includes both never giving up and realizing that you have to put forth the work if you want to get better. Malcolm Gladwell's book *Outliers* provides a fascinating investigation into what separates the average from the exceptional. Although there are many factors that contribute to this divide, the most critical one is effort: putting in the time and working to get better. As someone who is interested in becoming an exceptional leader, you should find this very encouraging. If you focus on acquiring the ability to lead by understanding and then applying the information contained in this book, you will become a better leader.

THE LEADERSHIP JOURNEY

The most dangerous leadership myth is that leaders are born—that there is a genetic factor to leadership. This myth asserts that people simply either have certain charismatic qualities or not. That's nonsense; in fact, the opposite is true. Leaders are made rather than born.

—*Warren G. Bennis*

Unlike other books, which present different examples of leadership or different philosophies of how a leader should act, this book cuts to the chase: it gives you what you need to know to become an exceptional leader and then provides you with an actionable plan. The purposes of this chapter are:

1. To help you identify what you want your leadership journey to look like, and
2. To introduce a map to help you along your way.

Have you ever been on a road trip? Just gotten in your car and taken off without any particular destination in mind? Felt the excitement of driving on a new stretch of road and passing small towns you wouldn't have otherwise seen? Taking off like this can be a great experience and one that can help you gain new perspectives on the world and your place in it. The goal is the journey: the call of the open road, experiencing new people and places, and learning more about yourself in the process. This sort of road trip is a journey-based experience.

Alternatively, I'm sure you can think of times when you have had a specific destination in mind. You probably had a particular place that you needed to be at a particular time, and you, therefore, made sure you could accomplish your goal. You figured out which roads you needed to take and about how long the drive would be, and you planned accordingly. This is an example of a destination-based experience.

Most leadership books tend to fall into one of these two categories: they depict leadership as either an ongoing journey with a very personal but non-specific outcome or as a destination that looks and acts a particular way. Journey-based and destination-based approaches are both important and can be appropriate. In this book, we will tend to refer to leadership *development* as your leadership journey. Your destination is the leader you want to become.

So what's missing? Well, journey-based and destination-based car trips both assume that you know how to drive. This is a simple observation, but it is important to recognize. If you don't know how to drive, the ideas and descriptions of either approach are going to be confusing and probably overwhelming. Similarly, many leadership books assume you already know how to be a successful leader. (By the way, when we refer to "success" as a leader, we are specifically referring to how *you* would define successful leadership, not how we or anyone else would define it.)

George Marshall is an example of someone who invested the time necessary to be an exceptional leader — and to know who he wanted to be as a leader. Today, we know General George Marshall as one of the pivotal characters of World War II. He is remembered for creating the European Recovery Program (also known as the Marshall Plan) and credited for helping post-war Western Europe rebuild and recover. Before he emerged as an exceptional leader, General Marshall spent many years in the military in relative obscurity. He was not a highly visible leader like his contemporary, George Patton; however, he knew who he was and what sort of a leader he wanted to be, and he used this vision to gain insights and experiences. When presented with an opportunity, he used his sense of self and his decades of acquired leadership ability to be exceptional. It would have been impossible for General Marshall to create his plan without first developing the foundation for success. We all crawl before we walk, and we walk before we run. General Marshall is a great example of why you must build upon a solid foundation of skills and abilities before attempting more advanced achievements.

Going back to our driving examples, think about all the work that went into building your ability to drive a car. You weren't able to just decide one day that you were ready. Instead, you had to build up enough skill to become proficient, competent, and not a danger to yourself or others. There were probably drivers' education classes and written tests. When you first started out, you likely spent hours with an experienced driver in the passenger seat coaching and directing you. Only after your skills increased and you passed your licensing exam were you given the privilege of driving independently.

Try to remember the first time you drove by yourself. Was it exciting? Overwhelming? A little scary? Suddenly, you were responsible for a machine capable of taking you from place to place — a machine you could direct and which could be both a useful tool and something highly enjoyable.

Now think about your journey to becoming a leader. Did you develop a specific foundation that you then built upon? The vast majority of business, political, and social leaders we have worked with have said time and again that they did not. Most leaders simply jumped in, tried to learn along the way, and eventually figured out what worked and what didn't. As you can imagine, this approach was successful for some and unsuccessful for others.

Think about the first time you had to turn across traffic. Depending upon where you learned to drive, this could have been a terrifying experience. Oncoming traffic speeding directly at you, the risk of someone coming up behind you, the need to check your mirrors constantly, and then to find that perfect moment to commit, hit the accelerator, and hope to make it across the street successfully. It would have been tough at first but, over time, probably became less stressful. You learned to manage all of the input and motions (checking mirrors, gauging oncoming traffic, knowing of your vehicle's acceleration, etc.) Eventually, the process became second nature, something that you could do automatically. You developed the skills and abilities necessary for this because you worked at them.

Now imagine that after your first attempt or two to turn across traffic, you decided that, because it was stressful and felt uncomfortable, you were simply never going to do it again. Instead of making one left-hand turn, you always made four right turns to arrive at the same end point. While this is technically possible, it's terribly impractical and inefficient; however, it is exactly what many of the leaders we've worked with have done. They tried something early in their leadership journey, found that it was stressful or uncomfortable, and decided they were never going to try it again. In driving, it's easy to see how unnecessarily complicated and difficult life would be if we always made four right-hand turns instead of one left, but this sort of thing can be harder to recognize in leadership. We have trouble getting past the idea that if something doesn't come easily, it's not worth developing.

Before continuing to read, please take a moment to reflect on your journey as a leader. Perhaps you are a high school student just starting out, thinking about what it is to be a leader. Or maybe you are a CEO of a multi-national organization employing thousands of individuals.

We all have a preconceived notion or existing mental model of leadership, and it will be impossible for you to get the full value of this book if you don't acknowledge your current perspective and open your mind to the possibility of change.

As educators, we know that if someone does not want to learn, they won't. If someone wants to find a reason not to believe, they will. If someone thinks something is not worth doing, they won't put forth the effort. However, our research has shown that anyone who puts forth the effort to learn our leadership approach will improve. Anyone who thinks they have something to learn will learn something new and valuable. And, most importantly, anyone who sees the value of investing in their ability as a leader will receive a return on their investment through increased effectiveness and satisfaction.

When you are ready to continue on your leadership journey, please proceed to the next chapter.

THE FRAMEWORK

ACTION

Action is the foundational key to all success.

—*Pablo Picasso*

There are few things more important to the success of a leader than getting started and then continuing to show up. This is the root of action in leadership. It is not a highly complex concept, nor is it something that requires years of meditative study to understand.

Leadership is just a matter of getting up and putting forth the effort.

As humans, we have this amazing gift called free will. We always have the ability to make a choice. There are times when we might feel like we don't, but there are always choices. The real limiting factor is not choice, it is consequence. When your alarm clock goes off in the morning, you have a choice whether or not to get out of bed. Of course, if you choose to stay in bed, you will have to deal with the consequences — from your boss, spouse, kids, pets, and on and on. Even when we feel like we are not making a choice, we have made a choice. Avoiding action is choosing inaction.

In some cases, there may be a reason why making a choice is particularly difficult or unpleasant. Maybe the outcomes seem equally bad or it feels like a no-win situation. If you speak up in a meeting and your idea is not well received, you risk losing face and credibility. On the other hand, if you don't speak up, you are providing your silent consent for something you might not agree with — or worse, know is wrong.

In order to be an exceptional leader, you must embrace the concept of purposeful action.

Exceptional leaders take action in a purposeful way. They become effective at advocacy, assume leadership roles and increase their involvement, mentor others, network, engage in the political and civic process, and serve as a resource for others. Putting forth the effort to improve in these specific areas will have a direct and observable impact on your ability to act as an exceptional leader.

ADVOCACY

Advocacy is the first area of action. By advocacy, we don't just meant social causes, although that is where we see it most frequently. Think of advocacy as *applied passion*.

How do you create the sort of energy necessary to sustain an ongoing commitment to action as a leader? Try first identifying what you are passionate about and then applying that passion. For example, anyone who has spent a fair amount of time in the southern United States soon discovers that college football is an absolute passion there.

The Southeastern Conference, or SEC, is a group of large public universities located in the same general geographic area. In the fall each year, there is endless conversation around how SEC teams will perform and predictions of who will emerge on top in the division, and likely the nation. As the season continues, the conversation turns from predictions to justifications: why a heartbreaking loss was a good character-building moment, or how an injured player is the reason for a losing season. From a practical perspective, these conversations—this passionate debate—is what advocacy is about.

When we are passionate about an issue, we are more likely to do something about it. It is the reason why people watch teams play. It is why people pore over player statistics and listen to talking heads provide expert opinions on ESPN.

> *This is advocacy: increasing your knowledge to improve your ability to perform.*

In other words, when you want to be seen as knowledgeable about a topic, take the time to learn about the topic, and then look for opportunities to share your increased knowledge and ability. That is advocacy.

You don't need to be passionate about or an advocate for everything in life. But you do need to find some passion somewhere. You need to learn to recognize when you are engaged and when you are going through the motions.

As humans, we have this amazing ability to develop muscle memory—i.e., programmed physical ability. If we focus on an act and work on the act repeatedly over time, it becomes automatic. Muscle memory can turn advocacy into a habit. It goes like this: you find something you are passionate about; then, you need to do something with that passion, such as having conversations, posting a comment on an online discussion board, or simply taking a few minutes to note your thoughts in your journal. The more you do these activities, the easier advocacy becomes. The easier advocacy becomes, the easier it is to harness it to take action as a leader.

So what is your passion? It doesn't have to be sports. If you find that you have a passion for breeding or showing dogs, do something with that. Love the outdoors? Get out there! Interested in the latest musicals or Broadway shows? Attend them and then engage with others about what you liked and didn't like. Love growing things? Plant something, nurture it, and talk to others about the process. No one can or should dictate your passions; it is your job to find out what you are passionate about and then do something about it!

The more you develop your advocacy muscle memory, the more you will find yourself performing as an exceptional leader.

ASSUME LEADERSHIP ROLES AND INCREASE INVOLVEMENT

What's a good step to becoming a leader? Drumroll, please...

Volunteer to lead! It sounds simple, because it is. The reality is putting yourself into a leadership role is what separates *wanting* from *becoming*. Wanting to become an exceptional leader is an important start, but it won't go anywhere if you never do anything with it. There is simply no substitute for experience!

A few years ago, we were working with a very large service organization with thousands of employees and hundreds of senior executives. To reward their top performers, the organization hosted a huge multi-day gathering where these exceptional individuals had the chance to engage with one another, hear from amazing speakers, and generally get more energized about going out and continuing to provide exceptional work. This was the upper of the upper in an extraordinarily competitive, highly regarded industry. Most if not all of the attendees commanded six-figure salaries, had large teams of direct reports, and were in charge of millions of dollars in annual budgets.

By almost any account, these individuals were not only leaders, but exceptional leaders. However, a funny thing happened during the gathering. During the sessions and seminars, the first few rows of seats were almost always empty—or partially filled at best. Being naturally curious, we decided to ask some of the participants not seated in the front why they chose to sit where they did. We received a range of answers, including the very honest, "I'm just not that interested" and "I have an important call that I will need to step out for mid-way." But the response we heard time and again was that people either didn't feel comfortable moving to the front, or they felt like those seats should be held for more senior leaders.

In an industry known for producing leaders, in an organization regarded as one of the top in the industry, and amongst the top of the top within this organization, we were hearing that individuals did not feel ready or qualified to lead. What a revelation! Good, bad, or indifferent, the reality is that most if not all of us struggle with feeling we are not ready or good enough. These are the feelings that supercharge our imaginations and our fear of consequences.

You have probably heard some birds will push their young out of the nest when they think they are ready to fly. While we are not proposing that you throw yourself into a leadership position if you feel you are really not ready to do so, we do suggest that sometimes you need to make a choice, put yourself out there, and have faith that you will learn how to fly.

One way to overcome the fear and doubt associated with taking on leadership roles is to change the way you think about leadership roles. Most people think a leader is the president or vice-president, a manager, or someone who has a title. This is not the case. Leadership can come in all shapes and sizes. Remember the words of Vincent Van Gogh: "Great things are done by a series of small things brought together."

Your leadership involvement can start with volunteering to do a task that you might not do otherwise. Use the experience to learn about yourself and who you are as a leader. Treat this as an opportunity to learn; success and accolades are a nice side benefit, but not the reason for taking the step. If you are a seasoned leader, it may be time to step forward and attempt to take on a more formal leadership title. Even if you are not successful the first, second, or tenth time you try, you will continue to learn more about yourself and, more importantly, better understand your journey to becoming an exceptional leader.

MENTOR

It is simply not possible to know everything about everything. Therefore, at some point you need to take stock and appreciate what you have to offer, rather than focus on areas where you might not be as strong. You will always be stronger in some areas than other people, and those are the areas you can teach.

When you teach, you usually learn as much, if not more, than those you are teaching. It is a classic win-win. As a mentor, you get to share your expertise and experience with a mentee; and as an added benefit, you get clarity and insights on both the topic you're teaching and on yourself and your leadership journey.

If you have little or no experience with formal leadership roles, you may feel you have nothing to offer a mentee. However, remember what we said about paying attention to your strengths. According to the dictionary, "Mentorship is a relationship in which a more experienced or more knowledgeable person helps to guide a less experienced or less knowledgeable person. The mentor may be older or younger, but have a certain area of expertise." So what do you know a lot about?

The reality is that in all likelihood, a younger individual with less experience in leadership roles may have significantly MORE experience with emerging technology, social media, or pop culture than someone older. Mentoring is not about being a sage on the stage, someone who shares wisdom accumulated over decades of experience. Mentoring is about sharing and developing, and through that process becoming a better, more exceptional leader.

NETWORK

Extensive research has been conducted on different personality types and preferences, and one of the most surprising findings is that there is no predictor of leadership success based on whether you are an introvert or an extrovert. Whether you have ever taken a personality inventory or not, this statement should make you think about what this means to your leadership journey.

Whether you like to meet new people and find that you are more energized after spending time with others, like an extrovert, or whether you find that your energy is drained after spending excessive time with others or meeting new people, like an introvert, your success as a leader is more dependent on your choices than on your biology. This is one of those choices: to recognize that leadership is a contact sport and requires you to put forth an effort to connect with others...or to decide you do not wish to put forth the energy to develop these important connections.

If the thought of networking makes you feel uncomfortable, take a deep breath and relax. We are going to start from the beginning so you can better appreciate this important process. First, we will provide a better understanding of what networking is and is not. Next, we will cover different networking strategies and approaches.

When you hear the word "networking," what is the image that pops into your head? Maybe you think of a dimly lit smoke-filled back room where politicians make deals in an unending series of political back slaps and horse trades. Or maybe you think of "working the room" at a function where you strategically make small talk with others while helping serve your own purposes. With these as two of the most common perceptions about networking, no wonder that it has such a bad reputation.

For those of you who don't meet new people easily, both of these scenarios can be horrifying. We often know that we should reach out and expand our networks, but doing so feels too difficult. Linking back to our discussion about choices: it is easier to choose to do nothing than to choose to make the effort and risk feeling awkward or embarrassed. What makes things worse is when we see others to whom networking comes naturally. Seeing them, it's tempting to decide that, since networking doesn't come naturally to us, we shouldn't even try—and before we know it, we are stuck in patterns that are preventing us from improving as leaders.

One of our biggest professional realizations around networking happened at a conference for high-performing executives. These individuals came from many different industries and backgrounds and were all extremely successful. On the agenda, there were several blocks of sessions that ran simultaneously. Executives could choose which session they wanted to attend based on their area of interest. Sessions ranged from the highly technical (for example, the proliferation of software as a service and implications for data centers and virtual hosting) to the very applied (for example, managing virtual teams). Each of the sessions was chosen by the conference organizers based on a specific demand from this group of executives.

One session that stood out was on practical networking. Of the available sessions, this was the least technical and, on the surface, had the least potential for impact. It was facilitated by a pair of consulting executives who had risen to be partners within their organization. Given the audience and the number of other really interesting sessions going on simultaneously, it might be hard to believe that the networking session was absolutely packed!

What an unexpected sight, a room full of executives who had already distinguished themselves as effective leaders choosing to spend their time learning about networking. The session started by the partners providing one of the most usable and coherent perspectives on networking we had ever heard:

> *"Most people think that networking is about getting something, which is why it tends to make us uncomfortable. The truth is that networking is about building mutually beneficial relationships. Knowing that you have something to offer can make all the difference."*

A very simple yet profound perspective.

The second point that the partners made was that too frequently networking feels like something that has to be done upwards. A junior individual has to make the effort to connect with those more senior than them. This power dynamic is another one of the reasons many of us are reluctant to put forth the effort to network. Generally, it feels like more work because we tend to perform or play a role when we are interacting with those who are more senior than ourselves.

Based on these typical perceptions of networking, one starts to feel a bit like Oliver Twist saying, "Please, sir, I want some more." What a ridiculous image! No wonder there are so many concerns and issues with networking! However, the two primary objections to networking—feeling like you are asking for something, and thinking that networking should always occur from the junior individual to the senior individual—are completely false. In order to break through some of the barriers to feeling more comfortable with networking, you need to get rid of these misbeliefs.

One of the best ways to eliminate misbeliefs is to replace them with positive perceptions. Like this:

Networking is not about asking; it is about being willing to give.

Networking is not about making the right connections, but on making meaningful connections.

Take a moment and think about the really authentic friendships in your life. You may have dozens of people whom you consider close friends, or you may have only one or two. Chances are, these relationships did not begin, and certainly would not have endured, if the sole point of the friendship was to get something from the other person. That is simply not how long lasting and healthy relationships begin! They begin because of mutual interest such as outdoor activities, sports, or shared childhood memories.

Friendships are healthiest when there is an ongoing give and take. Sometimes one friend needs support while the other is there to provide it. Other times the roles reverse, and on and on the cycle goes. We are not suggesting that networking needs to be seen as an attempt to make lots of new friends (although that might not be a negative thing), but that networking should resemble a friendship dynamic.

With a friend, you wouldn't mind asking for help if you needed it, because you know you would be willing to provide the same help to them if asked. You also don't have to worry about always trying to network up—friendships change and evolve over time. Sometimes you are at the same place at the same time; however, more frequently someone has had a bit more experience at something than the other and vice versa. Bottom line is that networking can, and should, happen up, down, and laterally. There is no secret recipe for the most effective form of networking; the key to becoming comfortable is to begin.

One more thing: relax! Take the pressure off yourself when it comes to networking. The worst thing you can do is to try and force something that feels unnatural.

In the sports world, you may have heard a player described as *playing loose*. This refers to the player's relaxed-yet-focused approach to the activity. What coaches and sports psychologists have found is that when players are *tight*, they fail to perform. Energy is spent on nerves and the fear of not performing rather than the task at hand. There are two primary ways that star athletes use to overcome these blocks: first, they develop a vision of how they want to see themselves perform; second, they develop strategies and a game plan to make that vision a reality. That's exactly what having the right perceptions about networking as a meaningful give-and-take can help you achieve.

Once you integrate this new and healthier vision of networking, the next step is to implement some practical strategies. We recommend three primary strategies:

1. Realize that you are networking already, and that this organic networking is the most authentic.
2. Develop a standard approach for those situations where you have to "work the room."
3. Practice and then practice some more.

The first strategy is to realize you are already networking and probably don't realize it. Whenever you do something, like start a job, volunteer, or participate in a sport, you can build relationships with those around you. You probably have something in common with the people around you. That something can be as simple as the activity bringing you together!

These possible relationships are seeds, and it is your job to plant, water, and care for them so they can sprout and reach their potential. This does not mean you should be schmaltzy or over-do it, but it does mean that you should make efforts to get to know individuals above and beyond what your job requires. You would be shocked at the network that you can develop over the course of a few years if you are intentional about it!

When we first started our professional careers, we had the opportunity to meet some really amazing people. We did not view these individuals as a means to an end; we just got to know some neat people who were going through a similar experience as we were at a similar time in their lives. Many years later, it is amazing to see where these individuals have gone, and the really fantastic things they are doing. Some have gone on to be C-Suite executives at some of the largest corporations in the world; others have become high-ranking officials in the government; others have become faculty and administrators at top universities; others have become entrepreneurs and stay-at-home parents. The point is not that we knew who would end up where; the point is that we made an effort to get to know people personally and have worked to stay connected over time. Now, as we have gone in different directions and ended up in different positions, we still have a relationship based on an authentic connection, not on a contrived desire to get something.

The key takeaway from the first strategy is that networking does not have to be forced; it should be natural. Start today by looking at those around you and making more of an effort to connect with them personally. You never know when you might be able to help one of these contacts in the future, or when you might need to call on them for assistance.

The second strategy is to develop a standard approach for when you have to "work the room." This can be a dreaded experience for those who are not comfortable with networking. A simple strategy is to start with something easy and work on gaining confidence over time. For example, if you are attending a large gathering where you don't know many people, think of a simple question or lead-in to help with the initial nerves of meeting someone new.

A few ideas to get the ball rolling:

- "Have you attended this event in the past?"
- "Did you enjoy the presentation?"
- "What keeps you busy when you are not attending events like this?"
- "Did you have to travel very far to get here?"
- "Where is your favorite place that you've traveled?"
- "Amazing weather isn't it? I can't believe it is still so cool in June! How is the weather where you are from?"
- "How did you come to be in your line of work?"

Here are a few additional suggestions to support the standard approach:

First, don't put too much pressure on yourself. Try to come up with one or two questions that you would be comfortable asking just about anyone and stick to those. If you actively listen and put effort into being interested in what the other person has to say, the conversation may take off. If instead the conversation starts to feel forced or awkward, give yourself permission to exit. "Great speaking with you. I hope you enjoy the rest of the event!" can be an efficient way to close a conversation without being inauthentic.

Second, look for situations that are approachable. If there is someone off by themselves looking highly uncomfortable, this might be a perfect opportunity to act as their savior and strike up a conversation. Chances are the person you speak with will be very grateful for your efforts, making them a receptive audience.

Third, set reasonable goals for yourself, and make your best effort to hold yourself accountable to them. For example, your goal may be to meet three new people at an event. As you attend events and gain confidence, perhaps your goal expands—or perhaps you find that you no longer need a goal because you are enjoying the process of meeting others. Having a goal helps because it gives you a target to work towards. Without one, this form of networking may feel like trying to boil the ocean—resulting in you shutting down and not making any effort.

Fourth and finally, practice and then practice some more. The more you practice, the more comfortable—and less anxious—you'll become. After all, before you stood up and walked, you had to learn how to sit up and crawl. Why do we do these things in this order? Because we need to learn the skills and develop the muscle control before we can master a complicated task. And keep this in mind, when it comes to networking: it's not about how much time you take to learn compared to other people. You might have only crawled for a week before walking, like our nephew, or you might have crawled for almost a year before trying to stand, like our daughter. Both are totally normal and totally appropriate.

> *There is nothing wrong with you if social situations make you anxious and nervous! The key to mastering social situations is taking small, manageable steps.*

This will make the process of developing the necessary skills and confidence easier. Whether you need to take a lot of time to network well or whether you are able to immediately network like a pro with little or no additional effort—that's great. Just be authentic to yourself, and, most importantly: *begin*.

Leading must be done with a personal touch, and networking is all about developing relationships that are mutually beneficial and established through personal effort. Therefore, as you become more and more comfortable and confident in your ability to network, you will find you are becoming a more exceptional leader.

EXPAND ISSUE ENGAGEMENT

One of the areas that differentiate average from exceptional leaders is the ability to apply leadership abilities in many different contexts. What we know from theory and practice is that it is absolutely critical that leaders be able to quickly assess and react to evolving conditions. For example, the leadership skills necessary to motivate a group of volunteers to complete a task is very different than those necessary to direct an emergency response team in a time of urgent need, like a natural disaster.

It happens all too frequently that, once we find something that works, we stick with it. One of the best ways to expand your thinking as a leader and to gain a perspective on different contexts and realities is to expand your engagement with, and knowledge of, different contemporary issues. Specifically, we suggest you become well-informed about contemporary economic, political, cultural, and social dynamics from a local, national, and global perspective.

A common error is to overestimate our abilities and expertise. Although it is important to have a strong sense of self and to believe in yourself, doing so can be dangerous when taken to an extreme. Put more succinctly: most of us don't know what we don't know. A purposive effort to build your expertise in multiple areas will help you overcome this issue. Many of the leaders we have worked with over the years have an innate curiosity and seek information naturally. However, many others have indicated that until they made a dedicated effort to be more engaged in the broader world of issues, they found it too easy to fill their days with other activities, like work, family, and entertainment.

Every day the world gets a little smaller and more connected. It is almost impossible to think of a situation where choices made at a local level are not somewhat impacted by national and global considerations.

For example, right now the price of a barrel of oil on the global markets is at one of the lowest levels it has been in recent history; however, there are signs that the price is increasing based on supply interruption issues around the world. There are almost an endless number of contextual considerations that a leader well-informed and engaged with this contemporary issue could make.

Even if global economic markets are not your area of expertise, an awareness of them might be very important. For example, if the price of oil rises, there will be price increases across industries such as transportation. If oil prices go up, so do gasoline prices. As gasoline prices increase, people drive less. If the trend continues, people become less inclined to purchase new cars, especially less fuel-efficient cars. Consequently, there could be a knock-on effect to the automotive industry. Similarly, if it costs more for a farmer to run their tractor, food prices will likely increase.

From a supply perspective, when oil prices are high, the economics of non-traditional oil pumping approaches become more favorable. For example, in the United States, increases in global oil prices are generally associated with increases in shale oil drilling and output. A consequence of this change is a larger workforce demand. Furthermore, there will be a need for support and supplies as new oil rigs come online and a need for housing and entertainment for newly employed oil field workers. Around the globe, oil prices may have a direct consequence on local political and cultural forces.

The point of the preceding thought exercise is not to advocate for leaders to become experts in economics, foreign policy, or social systems. The point is to demonstrate how there can be so many consequences from a single economic indicator, such as the price of oil. As an exceptional leader, part of your responsibility is to "see around corners"—develop intuition for what may be coming next and the potential consequences of it.

This intuition is an ability that must be acquired, just like any other. It is simply impossible to one day decide that you have now mastered an understanding of economic, political, cultural, and social systems. In fact, the more you invest yourself in learning about these systems, the more likely you are to realize that there is so much more to know!

To help you engage with the world, we have four main suggestions.

1. No matter where you are currently from an issue awareness perspective, you must decide you want to improve. This is the most critical first step. Both thinking you already know everything and thinking you are so far behind you don't know where to begin can be barriers to improvement.

Some of us have a natural curiosity that drives us to read the local newspaper every day, along with magazines and books, and to track the latest news on Twitter, BuzzFeed, and other online media outlets. At the other end of the spectrum, some of us do not engage in any issue awareness beyond celebrity gossip or reality television shows. Both ends of the spectrum, and all those in between, are completely legitimate places to begin this journey. The key to eventually getting to a level of engagement and expertise is to just *start*.

2. Define a very simple and achievable goal for yourself in this area. For example, your goal may be to skim one newspaper once a week or to watch one 30-minute news show once a week. The point is to come up with something that you can commit to and feel confident that you will follow through on. After watching a month's worth of shows, you will be more informed than before and will likely begin to seek out additional sources to supplement your issue engagement.

We don't suggest beginning by "drinking from the firehose." If you wanted to spend every minute of every day becoming engaged in different issues, the resources are certainly available. There are countless online and hard copy news outlets and, depending on your television package, you may have over a dozen 24-hour-a-day news channels. The risk of starting at this level of engagement is that it is rarely sustainable. You might be able to engage at a very high level initially, but once you start to lose focus and momentum, you will probably disconnect from the process completely. It's easier to sustain a small level of engagement.

3. Don't limit yourself to just one issue area. When we begin the process of engaging with issues, we might find that we are drawn to one particular area. Maybe we enjoy numbers, and so find economic systems interesting. Or we are fascinated by history, and so find political and cultural systems easiest to engage in. Or we love pop-culture and are fascinated by viral videos and online memes, and so are most drawn to social systems. It's totally acceptable to begin in any of these areas for any of these reasons.

When we learn something new, it is easiest to build upon our strengths before tackling our weaknesses. For issues, it is great to begin with something you are comfortable with, but it is also important to, over time, expand your horizons and try to become engaged in a wide variety of issues. Try to integrate learning issues into your daily routine. For example, if you begin your issue engagement journey by reading a local newspaper every day, you might start by just skimming the headlines. As you become familiar with some of the main ideas, start reading the articles in one particular session—perhaps business. Over time, start reading the articles in the other sections as well—Local, Global, Arts and Entertainment, Sports.

The purpose of starting slowly is to generate interest and curiosity in yourself. If it doesn't seem to be working after a month or so, try something different. Don't keep doing the same thing beyond about a month and expecting a different result!

4. After you have developed patterns that allow you to engage in issues across economic, political, cultural, and social systems, find issue outlets that present an opposing view to the one you affiliate with.

Why in the world would it be beneficial to seek out opposing points of view? Most of the time, once we get to the point where we have a functional knowledge, we are satisfied to continue with the status quo. However, at a certain point, growth in these areas will plateau. You can break this plateau by exposing yourself to contrarian perspectives, which will force you to think critically about what you are learning. We like to call this a "for us, by us" cycle. If the only issues you are engaged in are the ones directly in your area of expertise, and if the only information you are exposed to regarding these issues shares the same point of view as you, eventually you may become closed off to the possibility of alternate realities.

For example, if you tend to be politically conservative and all you are exposed to is information presented from a politically conservative perspective, chances are that at a certain point you will reach saturation where the only perspective you can process and understand is politically conservative. However, if you force yourself to move out of your comfort zone and learn about an issue from a politically liberal perspective, you will gain an even greater understanding and appreciation for the issue—and increasing your ability to be an exceptional leader.

But take caution! This technique only works if you are mentally prepared for it. There is a term in the academic literature called cognitive dissonance. This is a fancy way of saying that, as humans, we can believe two contradictory things at the same time. We might know smoking is harmful to our health, but continue smoking anyway (and maybe even delude ourselves into believing that smoking isn't bad for us, only for other people)—and that is cognitive dissonance.

A reasonable amount of skepticism is necessary, but unless we are really ready and open to different perspectives, all we will hear is what we want to hear. We therefore recommend to attempt this fourth and final suggestion until you have mastered the preceding three.

Our goal is to help develop exceptional leaders ready to take on the challenges of today and in the future. Part of being able to address these challenges is being aware of and engaged in current challenges and issues. Engagement should drive action. Issue engagement helps to provide the context for the exceptional leader. This awareness allows exceptional leaders to take the right action at the right time for the maximum result and benefit.

SERVE AS A RESOURCE

Sometimes, we need a trigger to make us do what we should have been doing in the first place. An exceptional leader is someone who knows how to apply their unique talents purposefully and, in so doing, serve as a resource to those around them.

There are many situations where you might find yourself able to serve as a resource, both personally and professionally. When a leader takes the time to understand their talents and become open to prospects, a magnetic ripple goes out into the universe of possibilities and returns with an opportunity to serve.

For example, while we were working with a group of volunteers on a local board, one gentleman indicated that he was in the middle of a website design certification course. One of the requirements for the course was to complete a website from concept through completion. He was enjoying the material and was on the lookout for opportunities to apply his new skill for the practicum. Upon hearing this, one of the other board members said that another organization that she was involved with, a charity that provided hearing devices to children with severely diminished hearing capacity, was considering a website redesign but didn't have the technical expertise to begin. Watching the opportunity appear and the connection be made was very powerful. Over the next few weeks, the gentleman helped the organization design and deploy their website—and he completed his course successfully.

The importance of serving as a resource, and the reason it is in the Action factor, is that you cannot sit on the sidelines and make a difference as a leader. You must embrace the mentality that everything you do should be for a purpose, and that purpose should be for the betterment of others. Serving as a resource tips the scales of reciprocity in your favor. It is a way to stack the deck and put yourself in a position to have your willingness to give returned to you many times over.

Another way to think about serving as a resource is as making deposits into a cosmic bank account. Generally, a deposit earns interest. Over time, if that interest is added to your original deposit, the next round of interest earned is even larger. You did not have to do anything; your money did not have to do anything. Serving as a resource provides the same type of returns; however, the benefit is accrued through experience, good will, and the satisfaction of using your talents in a manner that is beneficial to both you and others.

As Albert Einstein once commented, "Compound interest is the eighth wonder of the world. He who understands it, earns it...he who doesn't...pays it." Why wouldn't you want compound interest to work on your behalf? Availing yourself to opportunities and then making the choice to act upon opportunities is one of the most powerful ways to become an exceptional leader.

SUMMARY

Every day, the sun comes up, just as it has for millions of years and just like it will for millions more. There is comfort in the predictability. Predictability is the basis upon which we make plans and look to the future. Predictability is one of the foundations of our civilization; however, predictability was also selling buggy whips when the first car had rolled off the assembly line. Predictability is being analog in a digital world; predictability is the enemy of action.

There are many areas where predictability is not only comforting but also critical—the sun not rising tomorrow has much greater implications than this book, so let's keep everything in perspective! However, to transcend the chasm from leader to exceptional leader, you must embrace the idea that action is the antidote to predictability and complacency. It is up to you to choose your path. Action takes you out of your predictable and complacent comfort zone and forces you to adapt, grow, learn, and overcome. These are the hallmarks of the exceptional leader.

In this last chapter, we discussed the most effective ways to improve your action capacity as a leader. Yet it is not enough to read the words in this book and never put the suggestions into practice. Whether you decide to try one of the suggestions or all of them, the key is to *begin*. Once you have pushed yourself to take this first action, we think you will be surprised at just how much you are capable of. Acting as an advocate for something, assuming leadership roles, mentoring others, networking, expanding your issue engagement, or serving as a resource—these are six dimensions critical to becoming an exceptional leader.

The next factor we will cover is Change. Change is part and parcel with Action because any action will result in some sort of a change. As an exceptional leader, you will be able to effectively pair these factors to create a more powerful leadership approach.

CHANGE

Change is the law of life. And those who look only to the past or present are certain to miss the future.

—*John F. Kennedy*

There are few things that are utterly predictable. They say that only death and taxes are inevitable, but even these things reside in the bucket of change. Change is the underlying current in which we are all just passengers. It is impossible to resist change. Instead of avoiding it, therefore, the exceptional leader finds a way to harness change and use it to their advantage.

Change is like sailing. If our plan were to travel from Boston to the United Kingdom on a sailing ship, we would need three fundamental items: the destination (let's say the white cliffs of Dover), the vessel (an appropriate ship), and some way to power our trip (the wind). Without these three fundamentals, the journey could never begin.

Now, let's explore these three fundamentals in greater detail.

Destination: this can be any desired end-state or goal, personal or organizational. Without an intended port of call, the journey would make no sense. It would be like leaving Boston harbor and not knowing whether to sail north, east, or south. As the late Yogi Berra famously said, "If you don't know where you are going, you'll end up someplace else." As a leader, you must have some vision for the goal of the journey.

Vessel: this is you, the leader. It is your job to move from starting point to ending point and to carry the load as well as the passengers. You must be strong and capable and have the ability to travel great distances, weather storms, and maintain your bearing. Most importantly, you must be able to harness the wind to make the journey. Without the ability to unfurl your sails and effectively use the wind, your journey would be at best painfully slow. You would be completely dependent on the tides and currents to take you out of the harbor, into the open ocean, and then across the entire Atlantic to arrive at your destination—and you would most likely run aground somewhere very near to where you departed.

Wind power: this represents change in its most fundamental form. The wind blows whether it is harnessed or not. In much the same way, change is happening around us all the time, whether we acknowledge it or not. The wind is a perfect metaphor for change because we have all felt how much it can vary. The wind never blows strictly from north to south or east to west, nor does it have a predictable velocity—it can range from a warm summer breeze to a category five hurricane. Because it is both unpredictable but always returns, the wind can power a ship from one side of the Atlantic to the other just like change can power an exceptional leader.

As for a sailing ship, the winds of change do not always need to be at our backs for us to make progress. Through the process of tacking, or changing a sail to different angles, sailors can use the wind to make forward progress regardless of the wind direction.

In the next section, we will delve deeper into the four dimensions that underlie exceptional leadership within change. As you read about the different areas, we recommend you keep the sailing metaphor in mind. Specifically, think about each of the recommendations as a technical capability that, once mastered, can allow you to more effectively harness the winds of change. The more you can master these skills, the greater your ability to leverage the awesome power that change represents.

ACT AS A CHANGE AGENT

According to the Cambridge Dictionary, a change agent is "a person or thing that encourages people to change their behavior or opinions." We like this definition because it does not overcomplicate the concept. From our research, we have found exceptional leaders continually encouraging others to change their behavior or opinions.

Although encouraging others to change their behavior or opinions should be part and parcel with leadership, it doesn't always happen in practice. Like most of what we recommend and suggest throughout this book, the key is not intellectually acknowledging what one should do, it is being intentional: acknowledgement leads to action, and action leads to behavior, and behavior leads to cognitive integration.

Think it. Do it. Become it.

At this point, you likely have one of two responses to this call to action: either you already act and behave in this manner and therefore have the ability to act as a change agent fully integrated into your ethos; or, not being fully comfortable with the concept of acting as a change agent, you think, "This is interesting, but how in the world do I begin?"

Imagine the first time you looked at a specific painting. Maybe you noticed things like the canvas size, the colors used, and the frame it was in. The next time you looked at the painting, you noticed a greater level of detail, such as the artist's use of perspective, lighting, and subject choice. Subsequent viewings allowed you to see even more in the same work, including the influence of other artists and artistic trends during the time. The painting did not change between viewings; your knowledge changed, allowing you to see something new and different each time.

From this perspective...if you are in the first category and already have some mental models for how to act as a change agent, you can use the subsequent suggestions as catalysts to critically examine whether you have any areas to improve upon. If you fall into the second category, you can use the suggestions as a beginning and then move on to more complex situations as you learn. You should always use your experiences to guide the process and to ensure you can identify ways to integrate or improve your ability to act as a change agent.

We intentionally kept our recommendations at a very basic level, because the last thing that we wish to do is discourage anyone from beginning. You can start small and build comfortably from there.

One of the most effective ways to begin acting as a change agent is to create a new approach or idea. This idea does not need to be an earth-shaking epiphany. Instead, give yourself permission to start with something very small and well within your domain of control and expertise. The key is to make sure that whatever you come up with, you feel invested in the suggested change. For example, you might start with something small, such as how the dishes are loaded into the dishwasher at home. You have probably never thought about how dishes are loaded and thus never taken the time to think about the possible consequences of these actions. However, something as small as loading a dishwasher can have a large impact when you take a moment to consider a half-full load requires the same amount of water as a full load. This effect is multiplied when you think that each gallon of clean water that is conserved is worth approximately 10 gallons of water that need to be pumped or otherwise sourced. This is an area where you can create a new approach—maximizing the dishwasher space and only running it when there is a full load—encouraging others to change their behavior, and help conserve water in the process.

There are numerous other ways that you can create new approaches or ideas. A few other suggestions are: the mode of transportation you take to work, the type and amount of fertilizers and pesticides you use, and where you get the food that you eat. As an exceptional leader, you need to be aware that not everyone will be open and receptive to your suggested changes. In fact, some may be vehemently opposed to your perspective. The key to the exercise is to encourage others to change their behavior or opinions. The more you look for opportunities to create a new approach or idea, and then encourage others to change accordingly, the more comfortable you will be with the process. The more comfortable you become, the more likely you will begin acting as a change agent and embracing your role as an exceptional leader.

INNOVATION

One of the most frequent requests we get is to help establish a culture of innovation. This request always seems to be rooted in the desire to prevent stagnation and irrelevance. However, innovation is not a magic bullet that can be used to solve all ills; rather, it is a valuable tool that can be used appropriately to help individuals and organizations rise to new levels of excellence.

Positive innovation might be thought of as a strong tail wind of change. When innovation and destination are aligned, great progress is possible, but innovation that is not aligned with the desired destination may drive the ship off course and cause more harm than good. As an exceptional leader, your ability to harness and direct positive and productive innovation activities is critical. You must have a constant desire to encourage, support, and embody innovation while constantly checking to ensure the innovation is aligned with the anticipated outcome.

To develop a strong orientation towards innovation, we suggest a pragmatic approach. First, and probably most importantly, you must be open to new ideas. This is critical. You can't innovate without openness any more than you can run a marathon without getting out of bed. You simply cannot develop an ethos of innovation if you are not open to new ideas.

Frequently, we find people are not even aware of their internal blockage. You might have every desire in the world to go out and run that marathon; you might read about the process, purchase the necessary equipment, and mentally prepare for the endeavor. However, if you don't run it, it's just a mental exercise. The same holds true for innovation. You might read books, watch TED talks, and attend seminars to learn from experts; however, unless you are open to new ideas, it's just a mental exercise.

To overcome this obstacle, we suggest you prepare yourself for a bit of self-analysis. One of the recurring themes throughout this book is Greek philosopher Plato's "Know thyself." You can't begin a journey if you don't know where you are starting. As leaders, we must work to become more in tune with our thought processes and how we authentically experience the world. To assess your openness to new ideas, try keeping a journal for at least one week and tracking whether you were open to or dismissive of new ideas. These ideas can be in a work context, or social context, or a recreation context. The context is less important than the natural inclination.

In your journal, draw a line down the center of a sheet. On the top of one side write 'OPEN' on the other side write 'CLOSED.' During the day, every time you are exposed to a new idea or concept, do a micro-check of your first reaction to the idea. Place a tally under the appropriate header. This micro-check should be an intentional process for you to assess your initial reaction. At the end of the week, hopefully you have been exposed to at least six new ideas. Look to see if there is a pattern. If all your tally marks are in the closed column, it is likely that you are not cognitively open to new ideas and, by extension, innovation. On the other hand, if you have a mixture of tally marks in both columns, or most marks in the open column, you are cognitively open to new ideas.

If you found that most marks are in the closed column, we encourage you to spend longer monitoring your reactions to ideas. If the trend continues for over a month, it might be necessary to spend some time thinking about what's causing this block. Are there stressors in your life that are preventing you from being open to new ideas? Is there something from your past that's in the way? The more you can be mindful of your initial responses to new ideas, and the more you can objectively try to determine why you might be dismissive, the more likely you will be to change your immediate reaction and improve your openness.

Once you have verified that you are cognitively open to new ideas, we suggest you focus on challenging the process. Ultimately, innovation is about change, and change is about disrupting the status quo. Challenging the process is intended to do exactly this. As an exceptional leader, one of your roles will be to challenge those around you to think in new ways and create new approaches and processes. This might be taking a contrarian perspective or intentionally stirring the pot.

When a leader can agitate a situation in a positive manner, they can elicit more creative responses and thinking. We want to be clear, though, that we are not advocating you become a gadfly. As an exceptional leader, your responsibility is to challenge the process in a constructive manner, not to irritate those around you. To help begin developing your comfort with this process, we suggest adapting and using the following questions:

- What would happen if our assumptions about the _____ condition change?
- Is there the possibility that _____ could happen? If so, what would be the consequences?
- Is this an issue of resources or expertise?
- Are there any steps in the process that we can eliminate?

This is by no means a comprehensive list, but you get the point. There are always questions that can be asked. Even if the assumption is that everyone knows the answer, challenging the process can be an effective way to improve innovation.

A final suggestion for improving your overall innovation capacity as a leader is to intentionally seek to identify innovative solutions to challenges. At first, this may seem to be the sort of recommendation you would expect from the fictitious Department of Redundancy Department. However, the key to this proposal is the focus on intentionality. Returning to the idea of running a marathon: it would be reasonable to think that, prior to one day waking up and deciding to run 26.2 miles, you might want to train your mind and body.

This suggestion represents innovation training. The more you practice something, the more comfortable you become with the steps, subroutines, and processes involved. If you try to cultivate your ability to identify innovative solutions to challenges under non-critical conditions, you will be much better equipped to create and implement innovative solutions when the stakes are higher. These do not need to be the sort of monumental innovations that we can easily identify (for example, the automobile, air travel, the internet, and smartphones); they can be the sort of small incremental innovations that might impact only you and only on a very limited basis.

For example, one time we were down in Texas on a very large cattle ranch. In one of the barns, we noticed a series of ropes, pulleys, and weights. All these contraptions had small but important roles to play. A series of heavy gates had counterweights set up so that, after the cattle moved through the chutes, the gates automatically closed behind them. Overall, fewer people were necessary to perform the same amount of work, and the ranch worked cattle more efficiently.

We are not suggesting that you create a Rube Goldberg machine for all the different challenges you may encounter during your day; we are suggesting that you be intentional in developing your innovation capacity. Success tends to be built upon a foundation of failure. Your success in identifying innovative solutions to challenges will depend on your willingness to try—and likely fail, early and often. Accordingly, your overall capacity to identify innovative solutions will increase your overall innovation capacity as a leader, which will support your ability to master the change aspect of exceptional leadership.

RISK-TAKING

When considering the broader context of change, there are two different perspectives worth acknowledging. First, that change is a natural phenomenon, and that there will naturally be changes that leaders can, and must, be aware of and willing to act upon. Second, that as a leader, and as a human capable of making decisions and acting upon your own free will, you don't have to passively sit and wait for changes to happen to you. Instead, you can be the catalyst for change based on your willingness to take risks and try new ideas and approaches.

There are many situations in which you might find yourself at a leadership impasse. There might be social, political, environmental, or economic changes that are noticeable, but not necessarily having a direct impact on you or your leadership domain. As an exceptional leader, these are the pivotal moments where you must be bold and willing to take rational risks. We emphasize *rational*, because these risks shouldn't be reckless or foolhardy. There must be some consideration for both the costs and potential benefits associated with the risks. However, too much consideration can lead to a quagmire of analysis paralysis, where fear of making a wrong choice results in the choice of none.

To overcome the urge to overanalyze situations and cultivate a comfort with taking risks, we suggest starting small. Every day, we are faced with countless choices. Most of these are low stakes, but represent fertile ground for developing our risk-taking comfort. For example, how many times have you asked someone to go to lunch and then had the inevitable back and forth conversation of "I don't know what I'm in the mood for; what do you feel like?" Typically, after two or three rounds of "I don't know; where do you want to go?" a safe and predictable choice is made. This is the precise moment where you should exercise your willingness to be bold and take a risk. Instead of replying "I don't know," suggest a restaurant that neither one of you has ever been to. Who knows—you might find a new favorite place to eat.

Of course, there is always the risk of the new restaurant being underwhelming. This is where the rational aspect comes in to play. If you know you don't care for a certain type of food, it is probably best not to suggest that as an option! This same approach can be used on many other low-stakes decisions. Try watching a new movie genre, something that is totally outside your comfort zone. Instead of an action movie, try a musical. Instead of drama, try a goofball comedy. You never know where the minor risks you take will lead you; you could learn something about yourself or discover a new amazing place to eat.

However, this process is not just about self-discovery; it is about gaining practical experience taking risks and increasing your comfort level with increasing higher stakes decisions. At first, the worst outcome from your risk-taking might be indigestion after a bad meal or a wasted two hours spent watching a crummy movie. These negative experiences are valuable too, though, because they help you develop internal resilience and an experience reservoir. The more you work on becoming comfortable with the process of taking rational risks, the easier it will be to do so when you absolutely must.

Another outcome from these simple exercises is that you'll begin to see challenges as things to be mastered rather than avoided. This is another one of the differentiators between exceptional leaders and everyone else. Leadership challenges take many forms. These might be the macro-economic forces that we alluded to earlier. Anyone who had any sort of business interests for the last eight years knows exactly how overwhelming and helpless challenges of this magnitude can feel. However, no matter how dire or overwhelming a situation, an exceptional leader charges forward, willing to take risks to master the challenge rather than avoid it.

This is exactly the mentality Howard Schultz had as he took Starbucks from a four-store retailer in Seattle to the global powerhouse it is today. Being turned down by over 200 investors would seem like an insurmountable challenge to most of us; however, he learned and improved his approach with each investor. In the end, Mr. Schultz mastered these challenges and turned his four locations into more than 24,000 stores around the globe today.

The point of the Starbucks story, and the exercises we suggest, is to remember that chance favors the bold! Your journey to exceptional leadership will be well-supported if you become comfortable with taking rational risks. One of the most powerful ways we as leaders can improve our risk-taking mindset is to begin viewing challenges as something to be mastered rather than avoided.

SELF-EFFICACY

Depending on your background and previous experience with leadership development, you may or may not be familiar with the term "self-efficacy." At the most fundamental level, self-efficacy is *belief in your own ability to produce desired results*. That's it.

There are countless journal articles, books, and talks that cover this topic from all conceivable angles, and rightly so. This is one of the fundamental concepts in leadership and in life. However, like so many other concepts we cover in this book, the key to success is to keep it simple while focusing on the most important information rather than the minutia.

Believing in your ability to produce desired results empowers you to take control of situations regardless of context or the changes going on around you. Thinking back to our sailing metaphor: self-efficacy is the connection between the mast of the ship and the hull. The physical area represented by this interface might be small relative to the other more visible parts of the ship, but without a robust connection, nothing else on the ship will work. So too, self-efficacy can be one of the smallest yet most important interfaces between our desire and our ability to become exceptional leaders.

If the mast is sturdy and the sails are full, the winds of change can propel your ship to the desired port. However, if the mast snaps off, the ability to navigate and use the winds of change vanishes. Instead of having control of your vessel, you are at the mercy of nature. As an exceptional leader, one of your most important jobs is to focus on developing, protecting, and nurturing your self-efficacy.

Have you ever heard the Henry Ford quote, "Whether you think you can, or you think you can't—you're right"? This is the power of self-efficacy. You might have all the characteristics of a leader, developed the competencies of a leader, and completed the training necessary to be successful as a leader, but if you don't believe that you can be a successful leader, you won't be one.

There are many ways that you can go about developing and nurturing your self-efficacy. One of the most powerful tools to improve your self-efficacy is a positive mental image of yourself. This might be easier for some of us than for others, but we guarantee if you put forth the effort, you can improve in this regard.

To begin, know this:

Your life, no matter where you are currently, or what you have been through in the past, is valuable, and serves a purpose.

This does not need to be a spiritual purpose, but if you are comfortable seeing your purpose within a larger spiritual context, that is a great place to begin. For those who might be struggling with coming to terms with these entry conditions (that you have value and purpose) we pose the following thought exercise:

Imagine dropping a handful of sand on the floor and having a glass manifest. If you saw this happen, you would probably think the glass was very special and valuable. No matter what the glass looked like, it would be nothing short of a miracle. Now look at yourself in the mirror, and consider that the basic elements of the universe—such as hydrogen, oxygen, nitrogen, and carbon—have combined perfectly to create you. Miraculous! It is your responsibility to see yourself as a miracle every time you look in the mirror. Life is not fair, and change is not predictable; however, you are the manifestation of something very special and valuable. You have purpose. Your ability to internalize and fully integrate this belief into your mindset is critical to developing a robust self-efficacy.

As we empower you with this charge, we want to take a moment to clarify that this is not like flipping a light switch; deciding you are valuable and serve a purpose won't instantly give you a high level of self-efficacy. On the contrary, this will be an ongoing process where you may experience a great deal of initial improvement followed by backsliding, re-improvement, and ongoing maintenance for a long, long time. The key is to be mindful of your mindset and to continue to work on developing and nurturing it.

Once you integrate the belief that you are valuable and have purpose into your mindset, you will need to begin developing the belief that this purpose will become manifest through your actions. Purpose is not a passive activity. Purpose is the result of decisions, action, and willful change. When you can see how your purpose is aligned with your ability to produce desired results, your self-efficacy will be well-rooted. Even if things don't always go as planned, you will be able to see these minor setbacks as learning opportunities.

Although a whole chapter or whole book or whole series of books could be dedicated to the importance of self-efficacy, we don't want to get mired in the details here. As it relates to exceptional leadership, the most important thing to remember about self-efficacy is that it reflects your belief in your ability to produce desired results. To help establish this belief, we suggest starting by creating a very strong foundation, namely that your life is valuable and serves a purpose. From this purpose, your actions and choices will help manifest results through the various changes that you initiate or that occur naturally around you.

SUMMARY

Change is inevitable. It is a part of nature. As an exceptional leader, it is your responsibility to recognize, appreciate, and harness this change. You simply cannot be an exceptional leader by sticking your head in the sand and wishing for the winds of change to stop.

After recognizing and accepting the universality of change, your next responsibility is to prepare yourself to respond to change in an appropriate and beneficial manner. You will never make the journey across the Atlantic if you don't move into the open ocean and capitalize on the wind. The wind will not always be at your back; however, as an exceptional leader, you can use the winds of change to make progress towards your destination regardless of the winds' directions.

We just covered several different capacities necessary for excelling as a leader and learning to appreciate and harness change. It is your responsibility to take this knowledge and convert it to wisdom through purposeful and dedicated effort. Whether you decide to improve your capacity to act as a change agent, cultivate your innovation, take more risks, or develop your self-efficacy, it is up to you to act and improve your change capacity as an exceptional leader.

COMMUNICATION

The single biggest problem in communication is the illusion that it is has taken place.
— *George Bernard Shaw*

In one of our academic articles, we analyzed all the different leadership factors that have been proposed in the literature. After we grouped, sorted, combined, and clarified the factors, we discerned the higher-order themes that most academic representations of leadership include. One of the dominant themes is that leaders must be competent communicators. In fact, we successfully demonstrated that,

Communication competence is an entry condition to leadership!

Let us reiterate this point: to be a leader, let alone an exceptional leader, you must be a competent communicator. This is one of those revelations that shouldn't be a revelation, but frequently has the effect of an epiphany when you take a moment to contemplate it. Leadership by its very nature is a contact sport. It is not a solo activity done simply for the sake of self-edification. Activities that are done to improve oneself without interaction with others are for personal development. Personal development is a very worthy goal, but it is not leadership. To be an exceptional leader, you must interface with others; and the way we interface is through communication.

According to the dictionary, communication is "a process by which information is exchanged between individuals through a common system of symbols, signs, or behavior." As a leader, you will need to be comfortable using many different communication channels—oral, written, or non-verbal. You also need to develop communication capacities that are complementary to the delivery of information; specifically, you need to become a competent listener.

In the next chapter, we will analyze the four dimensions of Communication where exceptional leaders differentiate themselves. Depending on your leadership role—or the leadership role you aspire to—these dimensions might have more or less relevance for you. Our goal is to provide you with the knowledge along with the suggestions and recommendations necessary to develop your communication competence.

LISTENING

The most exceptional leaders realize that the key to success is to constantly work on developing the ability to better listen and, ultimately, to better understand. When a leader is conscientious about the need for and importance of good listening skills, they are well positioned to becoming an exceptional leader.

To become a great listener, it is important to appreciate and integrate the observation that the Greek philosopher Epictetus made: "We have two ears and one mouth so that we can listen twice as much as we speak." Leaders tend to feel the need and obligation to impart their wisdom and observations with others in a much greater quantity than they receive. However, we have found that the most effective leaders are those who are very intentional in their desire to listen and to appreciate what they are hearing.

The key to appreciating what you are hearing is active listening. It is not enough to simply quietly wait for the other party to finish speaking so that you can respond and speak yourself. This is passive listening and is not what we are suggesting. The keys to effective active listening are your level of engagement and desire to understand what the other party is trying to convey. This includes actively tracking not only the words that are said, but also the context, emotion, and underlying intent.

Given the ubiquitous nature of active listening advice, we don't want to dwell too much on the concept. It is very likely that you are already familiar with the idea and are probably more interested in how to become a better active listener than on the characteristics of active listening.

To begin developing a disposition toward active listening, we suggest doing an assessment of where you are currently. Try to monitor your conversations over the course of a normal day. Allow yourself to act in your most natural conversation pattern; this is not the time to begin working on your active listening skills. Instead, this is the time to determine where you are starting. After every conversation you have throughout the day, ask yourself:

1. Who spoke more, the other party or me?
2. What was the other party trying to convey?
3. Was I thinking of a response while the other person was still speaking?
4. Did I ask any follow-up questions?

These four simple questions can be very helpful in determining your current level of comfort with active listening.

The first question should be very self-evident. If you dominated the conversation, and you do so consistently, it is very likely you are not allowing the other party an opportunity to contribute. You must be brutally honest with yourself here. You might feel like your insights are so important that it would be a disservice to others for you not to share them. However, for our purposes, the justifications of the outcome are irrelevant. After a day or so of tracking who speaks more, you should have a robust sense of your primary approach.

The second question—what the other party was trying to convey—is a check of your engagement with the conversation. If after the conversation is over and you have no idea what it was about, chances are very high that you were not actively listening and consequently not fully engaged.

The conversations you monitor should not be limited to those where you are acting in a formal or informal leadership role. In fact, you should monitor both professional and personal interactions to better understand your authentic disposition. If you can recall what was conveyed during every professional conversation, but none of your personal conversations, this is a warning sign. The reverse is also true: if you can't recall professional conversations, but can recall personal conversations with perfect clarity, it is very likely that you are not allowing yourself to fully engage in professional conversations. The key at this point is to defer any judgment while you make an honest appraisal.

The third question—was I thinking of a response while the other person was still speaking—is a higher level diagnostic tool. Think of a time when you have been texting with someone and they ask you a question. You might be in the process of typing your response and getting ready to hit send when you see that other person has started typing again. People typically respond in one of two ways: either first you finish your text and hit send or you wait to see what the other person is writing before you send your response. In either case, whether you hit send or wait, the visual cue causes you to pause and consider how you want to proceed.

Unfortunately, when we are having verbal conversations, we don't have the benefit of seeing when the other person has already started typing. As someone committed to developing your active listening skills, it is your responsibility to monitor if you have started mentally typing while the other party is still composing their response. The reason you must be aware of this tendency is that when you move on mentally, you are no longer present in the conversation.

The final question — did I ask any follow-up questions — is another measure of engagement. If you find that you are never trying to clarify or gather more information, how engaged are you? If you are not asking any follow-up questions, this is an area where you can very easily begin to develop your active listening capacity. We suggest you begin with setting a reasonable goal for yourself. For example, if after a day you found you had five conversations and asked no follow-up questions during any of them, your goal for the next day would be to ask at least one follow-up question during one conversation. This is such a small step, and one that does not need to be in the context of your leadership role. It is something you can implement during a very low-stakes personal conversation.

The day after that, you might want to expand your goal to asking follow-up questions in at least half of your personal conversations. Eventually, you might want to challenge yourself to ask follow-up questions in all your conversations regardless of context. The more you practice this skill, the more you will find that you are interested in the response. You will automatically become more engaged in your conversations and will find that you naturally dominate less, understand what the other party is trying to convey more, and focus more on what is being said.

Once you have developed your active listening skills to a point where you can engage in the conversation, synthesize what is said, and respond accordingly, you are ready for the next capacity of the exceptional leader: facilitating discussions. The reason that we have nested facilitation under listening is that listening is the core of facilitating. To facilitate something is to "Make it easier or to help bring something about." Facilitating discussions is about making conversations flow and helping elicit that which is intended to be conveyed. Exceptional leaders do this by knowing what questions to ask and to whom. They listen carefully to what is said and then use their experience, logic, and intellect to help stimulate the process.

To become an exceptional leader, you do not have to become a trained facilitator; however, you must be comfortable and competent in facilitating discussions. The greater your ability to draw out important perspectives and insights, the higher your likelihood for success.

PERSUASIVE SPEAKING

As the world continues to become more technologically equipped, there has been a shift in the channels leaders use to communicate—from letters to memos to e-mail to SMS messages to texting to whatever new method may be released soon. However, from the very beginning of our history as humans, we have communicated verbally. Exceptional leaders are those who can communicate persuasively, particularly when speaking. There are certain patterns, cadences, and nuances possible when speaking that are unavailable through our current written channels. For this reason, we recommend focusing on developing your capacity to speak persuasively and then applying the lessons and approaches learned to other communication channels.

When thinking about the great leaders who have influenced you, chances are they were compelling and persuasive orators. This is not to imply that you need to become the next Martin Luther King Jr., Abraham Lincoln, Mahatma Gandhi, or Winston Churchill; the point is to acknowledge that many exceptional leaders are also well versed in the ability to speak persuasively. The research we have conducted with thousands of leaders from around the globe has shown the ability to speak persuasively is one of the hallmarks of an exceptional leader.

One of the reasons it is so critical to acknowledge the importance of persuasive speaking is the risk of cognitive dissonance that we described previously. If you don't believe the outcome of something, you will spend your time and attention on the reasons why the premise is inaccurate. Similarly, many people dismiss public speaking as an important dimension because of an underlying fear of public speaking.

For every decision we make, we internally (and usually unconsciously) compute a cost/benefit analysis. Are the potential benefits associated with the decision worth the potential costs? As the most common fear amongst adults, more than heights, bugs, or flying, the perceived costs of public speaking for many people is daunting. Our strongest recommendation is to not let this fear and potential cost prevent you from beginning the process and working to become a more persuasive speaker.

To help get more comfortable with public speaking, we suggest starting very small and very slow. One of the worst things you can do is to put yourself in a position where you are out of your depth with a low chance for comfort and success. For example, volunteering to present a keynote speech at a meeting attended by 2,000 of your peers may not be the best way to develop your comfort with persuasive speaking. This method of jumping in to the water without knowing how to swim and then panicking and struggling to survive is exactly why so many people end up hating the water!

Instead, we recommend starting very, very small: try reading children's books out loud. There are a few reasons we recommend starting at this level. First, the words and themes are simple, so there is not the burden of jargon or technical language to trip you up. Second, these are not your words, so you will not have the urge to critique and edit the language as you go. If you are practicing with a speech you've written, you will inevitably have two themes in your head: first, speaking and gaining comfort with the process of public speaking; second, mentally editing the words in your speech. The key at this stage is to develop confidence around public speaking, not wordsmithing.

Another reason to start with children's books is that they are meant to be read aloud. There is a cadence and rhythm to the words that will help teach you to make your own speeches flow more naturally. Finally, hearing your own voice out loud is very important. You must become comfortable with how you sound; and comfort comes from repetition.

After you become comfortable reading children's books out loud by yourself, the next step is to find an audience. If you have kids, perfect! If not, find friends or family members willing to serve as an audience. To preempt any potential questions or confused looks, we recommend explaining why you would like their help and how their support is important to your development.

After speaking in front of small and known audiences, we recommend expanding your speaking pool. Libraries are always looking for volunteers to read during story time. This is the perfect low-stakes environment where you can build your confidence.

Once comfortable with the mechanics of public speaking, it is time to push yourself to speak on more professional and sophisticated topics. The key is to not forget the lessons you learned while starting out. Persuasive public speaking is not just about conveying the information; it is about stirring emotion and connecting with listeners. Pay attention to your cadence and tone. Don't forget the power of pauses and allowing the audience to absorb what you are saying.

Most importantly, give yourself permission to develop your own authentic style and approach to persuasive speaking. We recommend that you watch TED talks and YouTube videos to see how some of the great persuasive speakers deliver their material. These are tremendous resources, along with countless other books and training aids that have been produced to help you further develop your persuasive speaking capacity. However, an exceptional leader will have a style and approach that is uniquely their own. The most critical aspect to becoming a persuasive speaker is to just start and then build upon your experience.

WRITTEN AND ORAL COMMUNICATIONS

Written and oral communications take a unique set of capabilities. Persuasive speaking, especially in public settings, is a method for transmitting your thoughts and perspectives with others; written and oral communication competence is making sure that what you are communicating is logical and has meaning. As an exceptional leader, it is critical that what you write and what you say are coherent, appropriate for your intended audience, and have a positive impact.

The first characteristic of an exceptional leader's communications is that they are coherent. Have you ever received an email that rambled on for way too long and made no sense? Similarly, have you ever listened to someone speaking or giving directions and found it impossible to understand what they were trying to get across? Anything you read or hear that has an unclear message is an example of incoherent communication.

As an exceptional leader, one of your most powerful tools is your ability to impart necessary information clearly and unambiguously. It is your responsibility to develop succinct, clear, and memorable points. For example, consider the following statement:

"I know it has been difficult for everyone to really get behind this move onto our new software system. There were lots of different considerations that we had to think about when choosing a vendor, and of course there were lots of challenges once we selected someone to help us. But eventually we knew it was the right choice, because we know our business, and they are experts in what they do, so if we can all start working towards the common goal of making the new system work, that would be great. I want you all to know that I'm working hard to make sure everything is going well, but there will be unforeseen hurdles so it is going to be a long journey, but one that will be for the best."

Huh? Although you might not have been involved in a large software rollout in your organization, chances are you have heard something like this before. There is no clear theme, intended outcome, request, or call to action. An opportunity to coherently communicate has been missed. Instead consider a coherent alternative statement:

*"On behalf of myself and the rest of the management team, thank you all for your ongoing support of the new software rollout. Although we knew the process would cause some growing pains, and there would be some bumps along the way, we could not be more pleased with the extra efforts that you have put forward to make the process successful. In the next 30 days, we plan to have all the new modules available across our business units; and in the next 90 days, we will be fully transitioned to the new system. We are already starting to see a dramatic increase in our ability to forecast needs and get the sort of business insights we hoped for when we started this journey. This is a direct result of your efforts! Thank you

all and please continue to provide your insights so we can create the best system possible!"

Obviously the two statements are vastly different in their tone, clarity, and intent. The first is a rambling recitation of what went wrong and what is continuing to go wrong now and into the future. The second is a clear summary of the work done thus far, the plan, and the importance everyone has in making the process a success.

To improve the coherence of your communications, here are three suggestions:

1. Clearly state your intended purpose—the most important thing for your audience to take away—at the beginning. This can be one of the first lines in an email, or the way you start a scripted speech. In less formal situations, where you know you need to have a conversation with someone, this process will require you to take some time before the conversation to clearly determine what you want to accomplish. It may help to write your purpose and then develop your supporting points accordingly. The more effort you put into improving the coherence of your communications, the easier and more natural doing so will become.
2. Think about your intended audience. More precisely, make sure your messages are tailored to your audience. Working at a university, we see this all the time. In the university system, there is a culture of jargon and technical language that is expected and used as currency. However, to a member of the general public, this type of communication is almost impossible to understand. Know your audience!
3. Make a positive impact. As a leader, you have the chance to make a real difference in the lives of others. Making a positive

impact is not always about moving the dial on a grand scale; it is about acknowledging the amazing contribution everyone can make.

The more you cultivate a culture of gratitude and appreciation, the larger an impact you can make in the lives of others. Every time you communicate with someone, you have the chance to either build them up or tear them down. Even corrective communications can have a positive impact if done in an intentional way. To develop an orientation towards making a positive impact, we suggest focusing on the developmental aspects of each communication. The more you can help others connect their time, talents, and contributions to larger outcomes, the more likely you are to have a positive impact on them and their efforts.

MEDIA RELATIONS

Communication in leadership is mandatory. There must be some mechanism for leaders to convey their thoughts and vision to others. However, the environment that leaders are operating in today is very different than when the original research on the impact of communication in leadership began in the 1940s. There have been very few new models of leadership that specifically address these changes. Our experience has led us to identify effective media relations as a characteristic of an exceptional leader.

Generally, when we share the importance of media relations, responses range from flat dismissal to skeptical acceptance. One of the primary reasons leaders discount the importance of this dimension is the historical, narrow, and generally inaccurate perception of what constitutes the media. In the past, the media has been considered an independent entity where journalists and reporters seek to answer the who, what, where, why, and when questions. These individuals represented well-known mediums such as newspapers, radio, and television. Although this might have been an accurate description even at the turn of the new millennium, it is no longer sufficient today.

Today when we refer to the media, we need to be more inclusive of the new mediums. While print media, radio, and television are still relevant, they share the space with new and emerging forms of *social* media. At this point, all manner of mental light bulbs should be going off. The relevance of social media on leadership today is so obvious that almost anyone that has not been stranded on a desert island for the past 20 years can see it!

Exceptional leaders engage the media in two specific ways:

1. They are confident working with the media.
2. They avoid no-win situations.

Let's delve into these in more detail.

First, exceptional leaders are confident with both traditional and emergent media platforms. We are not implying that all leaders must become media relations experts; however, they must be comfortable with the media process and, accordingly, confident with their abilities.

For example, most of us are familiar with "gotcha" media reporting, where individuals are surprised on the street or in their place of business by a reporter and camera crew. Generally, what we see is the target of the piece running away or becoming irate with the reporter. These reactions are what make for good television or print copy or going viral online. It is human nature, when confronted with a threatening situation, to devolve into a fight or flight mindset. However, there is a third option, one that requires discipline. Experts at media relations know that as the subject of a piece, they control the message and the optics. The media cannot fabricate your words or actions. If you give them unflattering material to work with, such as running away and looking guilty, you have no one to blame but yourself.

Exceptional leaders use the knowledge that they are in control of their actions and message to their advantage and develop an inner sense of confidence when working with the media. This is not to say that getting your message across will always be easy; however, responding to the media is not the same as testifying under oath. You are not under any legal obligation to answer the questions that you are asked.

We recommend you begin developing your confidence in working with the media by 1) developing a positive message that you would like to convey and then 2) practicing redirecting unrelated questions back to your message. Although most of us will not be the target of a news exposé, this mindset is applicable under less threatening conditions as well. The more you can stay on message and present an air of authority and confidence, the more likely you are to have favorable results. Social media is an example of alternative platforms where television cameras may not be thrust in your face for comment, yet responding with confidence and staying on message can have a positive outcome.

As an exceptional leader, you should be aware of the potential benefits and costs associated with participating on different social media platforms. We recommend doing research on the various platforms and how others are using each platform to enhance their leadership.

Currently, some of the most popular social media tools are Facebook, Twitter, LinkedIn, Instagram, YouTube, Pinterest, and Snapchat. As technologies evolve and new players enter the market, these names will change, but the process will stay the same. Knowledge is power, and power is a foundation for confidence. The more you can understand how and why a platform is used, the more confidence you will have in your decision to engage or not.

If you decide to become active on one or more platforms, pay close attention to the second characteristic that exceptional leaders share regarding media relations: avoiding no-win situations. Social media has done immense good to democratize the media and remove barriers to getting one's perspective and opinions out. At the same time, it has made interactions more anonymous and less civil. Anyone can berate, belittle, or cajole anyone with a social media presence.

Dealing with these negative individuals, or *internet trolls*, can be time consuming at best and devastating at worst. As we recommended previously, one of the best ways to deal with challenging media situations is to remain on message and present an air of confidence. However, one of the least productive ways to respond to online critique or negative comments from a troll is to engage. There is a saying that you should never get down in the mud with a pig; you'll end up filthy and they'll love it. Engaging an internet troll is the epitome of a no-win situation. The more effort you put forth, the more likely you will misspeak or have something taken out of context. Sometimes it is better to acknowledge that not every interaction is going to lead to a positive outcome; therefore, it is better to conserve your resources and look for more productive opportunities.

Even though there are risks associated with engaging with the media, we remain very strong believers in the power of all forms of media and recommend that leaders improve both their traditional and social media relations. There is a growing need for leaders who are confident working with all different types of media, and exceptional leaders are those who can use the media to their advantage. Confidence with media relations is one of the critical competencies for the next generation of leaders.

SUMMARY

Without communication, leadership development is indistinguishable from personal development. Many of the characteristics that help us to live richer, fuller, and more fulfilling lives are what make a leader successful. It is only through the transformative power of communication that we can share these values with others and become exceptional leaders. If a tree falls in the woods and no one is there to hear it, does it make a sound? If a leader is not able to communicate with others, are they really leading?

To become an exceptional leader, you must work diligently to cultivate both your skills and your ability to communicate those skills. When you are able to provide direction and clarity, your skills are multiplied through the positive impact they have on everyone your message touches. You might not believe that you have what it takes to become a great communicator, or to hold an audience in rapt attention, but all you need is to begin intentionally. Over the years, we have seen otherwise capable leaders stall in their careers because they have failed to spend the time and effort necessary to develop their communication skills. Rather than focus on where you are currently, focus on how you would like to improve and to make a commitment to taking positive actions to make yourself better.

In this chapter, we revealed the four dimensions of communication that exceptional leaders develop and employ. As you continue your journey towards exceptional leadership, we challenge you to not stop at simply reading the words on these pages; instead, actively take steps to develop and improve these areas. The recommendations we provided are such that anyone at any level of experience can begin working to improve — starting today. As you practice and master these entry-level exercises, you should continue to push and expand your communication development. There are many great books, videos, and trainings available to help you to continue to improve. The key is a willingness to begin and a commitment to continue.

The next chapter elaborates on the importance of relationships and leader character. The interpersonal nature of leadership interactions is critical to understanding how to make communication more effective, especially when taking action and during times of change.

RELATIONSHIPS & CHARACTER

In matters of truth and justice, there is no difference between large and small problems, for issues concerning the treatment of people are all the same.

—Albert Einstein

At its very core, leadership is about relationships—the interaction between two or more people. Therefore, one of your most important responsibilities as a leader is to create, nurture, and protect your relationships with others. By recognizing and cultivating their own interpersonal traits and characteristics, exceptional leaders build exceptional relationships.

One of our lines of research deals extensively with personality traits and dispositions. We, therefore, want to make very clear at the beginning of this chapter that when we refer to interpersonal traits and characteristics, we are not referring to genetic or hereditary dispositions. As it relates to leadership, the interpersonal traits and characteristics we are referring to are those that anyone, at any time, under any circumstances can develop. We certainly acknowledge that through inherited traits you possess, you might find the different dimensions more difficult or simple to master than someone with a different set of inherited traits. The ease in mastering these dimensions is secondary to the necessity for acquiring them. You must have this perspective as you begin your exploration of interpersonal traits and characteristics. If you don't have the right mindset, the first time you encounter a challenge, you will be tempted to disregard it as unnecessary.

Frequently, we've had leaders indicate to us they are simply "not a people person." This is like saying you are a swimmer, but don't care for the water; it is not an acceptable answer if you ever wish to become an exceptional leader. In fact, we would suggest that the only way to become a truly exceptional leader is by mastering the interpersonal aspects of the role. Interpersonal traits and characteristics are so critical to effective leadership that there are many leadership theories that reside only within this area.

In this chapter, we will cover the nine different dimensions of relationships and character that exceptional leaders embody: confidence, empathy, ethics, initiative, integrity, life-long learning, motivation, self-awareness, and understanding and appreciating diversity. When leaders develop and harness these traits and characteristics, they develop stronger and more resilient relationships with others. In turn, stronger relationships lead to better and more predictable outcomes.

CONFIDENCE

One of the defining characteristics of an exceptional leader is confidence in oneself and in one's abilities. Per the dictionary, confidence is "belief in oneself and one's powers or abilities." At the root of confidence is a certainty that you are up to the task. As a leader, this does not mean that you will never experience moments of doubt or find yourself questioning your ability to do something. It means that, overall, you feel knowledgeable, prepared, and ready to step forward into leadership roles when opportunities present themselves.

ISSUE LEADERSHIP

Think about the following scenario. After feeling a little sluggish for a couple of weeks, you finally go in to see your family physician. Your doctor listens to your chest and heart and thinks he might hear something that would explain your persistent lack of energy. He refers you to a heart specialist to have a few more tests. You reluctantly schedule the appointment with the cardiologist because you know it is important and the right thing to do, even though you are nervous about the possible outcome.

The cardiologist runs some tests. They hook you up to a bunch of wires and monitor your heart using an EKG. Next, they perform an Echo using an ultrasound machine to look at your heart function. After all the tests, you find out that you have a previously undiagnosed heart murmur. While on the spectrum of all possible heart conditions, yours is in the low-risk range, it will still require an open-heart procedure to repair. Along with your cardiologist, you decide that the best course of action is to schedule surgery soon so you can prevent further damage to your heart and hopefully go on to live a long and healthy life.

Your world has been thrown for a loop. When the day arrives, you meet with the cardiac surgeon to discuss the procedure and make sure that you are comfortable with the next steps. When the surgeon enters the room, you notice some intangible qualities: he moves with a purpose but is not hurried. He takes the time to listen to your questions while looking you in the eye and then patiently responds, making sure you fully understand what he has said. He uses language that is not scary or full of medical jargon. He is transparent with both his level of success and the risks associated with this type of procedure. At no point during your meeting do you feel rushed, ignored, or otherwise discounted. He answers your questions with ease and is decisive with his plan. At the end of your meeting, you feel much better and more prepared for your upcoming surgery. You know the surgeon is qualified, capable, and able to do a superb job. There is no question that he has the knowledge, is well prepared, and is ready to lead when you undergo your procedure.

The reason we spent so much time walking through this scenario, and the reason we know so much about how heart conditions are treated, is that it is something that we have experienced first-hand. We can say definitively there is no way that you can prepare yourself for something like this. In some ways, it is a very appropriate parable for the dynamic of a leadership relationship. As a leader, just like as a surgeon, one of the most important roles you have is to not only be confident in yourself, but also inspire confidence in your abilities with others.

After our meeting with one of the top cardiac surgeons in the world, we knew he was absolutely the right person for the job. He was the embodiment of confidence and self-assurance. However, and this is a key point, he was never overconfident and arrogant. The fine line between confidence and arrogance is one of the defining characteristics of an exceptional leader. The ancient Greeks had a term for overconfident arrogance: hubris. It was usually hubris that called down the wrath of the gods and served as a cautionary tale for others. The Bible also cautions against such behavior: "Pride goeth before destruction, and a haughty spirit before a fall"—in other words, "Pride comes before the fall."

At the other end of the spectrum, if the surgeon had come in and been unable to answer our questions with authority or with eye contact, we would have questioned whether he was someone with the presence necessary to command his team when a life was on the line. All his training and certifications would have meant nothing to us without his confidence.

We want to follow people that inspire us to have confidence in them. This is almost impossible to do if someone does not have confidence in themselves.

Ultimately, the level of confidence that you present should be determined by your internal barometer. There is not an ideal level of confidence that research has determined works best under all conditions. Instead, there are practical guidelines that you need to contemplate and then use to decide what is right for you. As an exceptional leader, your level of confidence should be neither meek nor arrogant. You will never be an exceptional leader if you cannot inspire others to have confidence in your abilities. At the other end of the spectrum, you might be able to convince people to follow you if you are overconfident and braggadocios; however, these leaders inevitably fail and lose the confidence of their followers.

To develop an appropriate level of confidence in yourself and your abilities, we suggest you begin at the foundation. Confidence is based in knowledge. The more we know about something, the less scary it becomes. If we are not scared, we are willing to be bold—and boldness is a hallmark of confidence. If you do not feel like you have the requisite knowledge, you need to work on acquiring it now.

If you feel like you have the necessary knowledge, you need to make sure you are prepared. Preparation is the step beyond knowledge. It is when you have taken the time to apply the knowledge in a practical way. When medical students are learning new techniques, they use a saying: "See one, do one, teach one." Now is the time for you to *do one* and *teach one*. These activities will help cement your knowledge and make sure that you are prepared. Look for low-stakes environments to begin practicing your leadership, and you will be amazed at how quickly your confidence follows.

Finally, you must be prepared to step forward into a leadership role if an opportunity presents itself. Confidence is great as an individual trait, but it becomes exponentially more powerful when applied in a leadership context. If you can harness your knowledge and preparedness and take on leadership opportunities with confidence, you will be well on your way to becoming an exceptional leader.

EMPATHY

As humans, one of the most powerful connections we share is our ability to relate to the experiences of others. This is the fundamental core of empathy as reflected in the dictionary definition: "The ability to understand and share the feelings of another." As an exceptional leader, empathy is necessary to create the sort of personal connections that enable you to achieve more than could be otherwise possible.

Empathy is one of the primary tenants of many leadership models, such as emotional intelligence and servant leadership. From all our research, we can confidently assert that empathy is one of the critical characteristics necessary for leaders to be successful in developing interpersonal relationships. These relationships are the foundation for building trust and being able to build consensus and marshal the efforts of others.

The textbook definitions of empathy are necessary because they help create a common language and understanding; however, we like to think of empathy in leadership as something even more fundamental. We suggest that, as a leader, you think of empathy as your responsibility to see, value, and honor the humanity of everyone you interact with and to always remember to treat everyone as a person first. From our research in personality, we know that some have more of a natural disposition towards empathetic behavior; but everyone can be proactive and improve in this area.

Across many of the different factors and dimensions of leadership that we cover in this book, empathy is one that has some of the most personal meaning. It is meaningful because it is a leadership lesson one of us had to learn the hard way. We have found that sharing our own experiences is one of the most powerful ways to convey the importance of these leadership lessons. The following is Kevan's experience as it relates to an early lesson learned around the importance of empathy:

Early in my career, I was working for a large global consulting firm. Specifically, I was working with client organizations to develop training material for their internal teams and external customers. I had the opportunity to build my instructional design and development skills and had a great deal of success getting projects out on time and under budget. As is the case in many large up-or-out organizations, I found myself on the fast track to management, with each project leading to more responsibility.

After a few small co-led projects, I finally had the opportunity to manage a dedicated team for a new client. It was an exciting chance to demonstrate what I could achieve. I had a team of four developers along with some part-time media support. One of my team members was an outside contractor named Charles. Charles had some great technical knowledge, having developed similar training materials for other companies in the past.

As is typical for these sorts of projects, the client was very anxious to see finished courses as soon as possible, because they were using the training to support the rollout of a new software system. Charles quickly became the team in-house subject matter expert as well as being responsible for completing his own work. He was a great guy who was knowledgeable and friendly; he was a huge asset to the team.

One morning as Charles entered the office, I noticed that something was different. His smile was bigger than usual, and he seemed to be glowing. When I had a chance to talk to him in the break room he couldn't wait to share the news that he and his wife had just found out that they were pregnant and expecting a baby! He was a neat person who worked hard and seemed about as happy as a person could be, so I was happy for him.

Over the coming weeks, the team continued to work hard and made very good progress on the training. The client was pleased with what we were producing and everything was on track for an on-schedule delivery. During the last two weeks of our project everything became incredibly intense. Final reviews and last minute updates were happening. Everybody was working hard to make sure that everything went off without a hitch.

I can still vividly remember that Tuesday morning when Charles walked into the office. He looked as though he hadn't slept at all, and his eyes were hollow and red. Whereas before it had seemed like his feet barely touched the ground while he walked because of his joy, now it was as if his heavy footfalls carried the weight of the world with them. It was clear that something wasn't right, but this was a big day for the team. We were in the final push to get everything done and handed over to the client. I saw Charles head to his desk and then became engaged in some urgent matter.

After about an hour or so, I asked Charles to step into a conference room so we could quickly touch base. I wanted to make sure everything was all right, but I also wanted to make sure that everything was on schedule. When I asked Charles what was going on, he looked up and said, "Last night my wife was killed in a car accident."

It was almost too much to even comprehend. Here was Charles, who just a few weeks earlier had been so buoyant over the news of their pregnancy, now facing one of the most overwhelming situations imaginable.

I tried to maintain my composure and told him how sorry I was and that if there was anything at all that he needed to please ask. I'm ashamed to admit that I then quickly followed up with a question as to whether he thought he would be able to finish his work up for the project. In typical Charles fashion, he said he would certainly try and headed back to his desk. Shortly after lunch, Charles indicated that he was having trouble focusing and needed to head home.

That was the last time I ever spoke with Charles. Obviously, the shock of the tragedy had impelled him to come to the office, but as the reality set in, it was more than he could bear.

Without knowing whether Charles would return, I assembled the team and reallocated his work. We would all have to work extra hard, but we could still make the deadline. That is just what we did: we focused on the work and pleased the client. The next week, we heard from Charles's contracting agency that he would not be returning. A few months after that, some of my team members shared that he had sent an email letting them know that he was all right and had found a new project that he was working on.

As the whole situation unfolded, I knew that I was not handling it as well as I could, but I justified my actions by focusing on the work and the needs of my client. As time moved on, however, I developed deep regret over how I'd acted. In retrospect, my lack of empathy was shocking. Now, more than 15 years later, I still feel the pain of how poorly I handled the situation.

Instead of focusing on the work first, my obligation as a leader and a human was to Charles. I should have offered him more than words; I should have given him the support and kindness he needed. Over time, the work has faded, and the projects and the deadlines met or missed have blended together. But my lack of empathy in that situation remains. My memory of it is something I carry with me every day, and I use it as a reminder to be intentional about developing and using my empathy to guide my thoughts and actions.

The silver lining for me is that I learned from this experience, and my life and leadership have benefited. For me, the lesson is that life is not fair. There are things utterly beyond your control; your job is to realize that although you can't control these situations, you can control your actions. You can choose to honor and respect the humanity of those around you. You can choose to live an empathetic life and to remember the importance of the connections that you share with others.

Although self-reflection can be painful, it is one of the most powerful ways that we have to learn the importance of empathy. Sometimes, it is easier to understand a concept by seeing the absence of the concept. If you can constantly remember the humanity of those that you interact with, you will become more empathetic. The more empathetic you are, the easier it will be to respect the thoughts and opinions of others. Likewise, the respect you give will be reciprocated through greater trust and openness. With greater openness comes a greater capacity to empathize with others. The self-reinforcing and perpetuating nature of this cycle will help to fully integrate empathy into how you act as a human and will help propel you along your journey to becoming an exceptional leader.

ETHICS

No doubt you are familiar with some of the recent public ethical failures in leadership: Enron, Tyco, WorldCom, Andersen Consulting, the sub-prime mortgage meltdown, and on and on. Recently, Volkswagen was found using software to cheat emissions tests. There have been entire books dedicated to the most noteworthy failures.

The point is, ethics and leadership have not always been synonymous; but we contend that to be an exceptional leader, you must be ethically grounded. In this section, we want to focus on how exceptional leaders use ethics to guide their thoughts and actions. We want to help you develop your own ethical framework to use as a leader—when times are easy as well as when they are challenging.

Unlike other leadership models or theories or suggestions with flexible perspectives on ethical behavior, we would like to clearly state at the beginning that to be an exceptional leader, you must view ethics as binary:

Either you are ethical as a leader or you are not.

There is no room for confusing and self-deceiving notions such as moral relativism. It is not sufficient to be ethical most of the time; ethics must be pervasive and constant in everything you do. You would not consider yourself to be an ethical person if you only robbed a bank occasionally; there is no credit accrued for not robbing banks all the other times you had the opportunity. And yet somehow this is the perspective some unethical leaders take, claiming, "My behavior, no matter how unethical, should be overlooked because of either my intent or all the good work that I have done." Nonsense!

As a leader, you are held to a higher standard. This is not to imply that you are expected to be perfect. We all make mistakes and have lapses in judgment. However, you must be 100% clear that these transgressions are not excusable and should not be rationalized. If you are not prepared to form this line of demarcation, we recommend that you research and contemplate the implications before proceeding. Not being prepared to make this commitment is like failing to make sure your parachute is properly packed before jumping out of an airplane. It is simply foolhardy. If you are not fully prepared to open your parachute — don't jump! Because you don't want to try and correct the situation on the way down. When you are presented with an ethical dilemma and you pull the rip-cord on your cognitive ethical framework, you want your parachute to deploy every time — because it failing to deploy will have a catastrophic effect on your leadership effectiveness and credibility.

If you are willing to accept the binary nature of ethical behavior, the next step is to clarify some commonly confused terms: ethics, morals, and values. There are entire branches of philosophy that contemplate these subjects, but we'll keep it simple with the following working definitions:

- *Values* are the internal guidelines we use to evaluate good and bad as well as importance. Values are our own internal compass based on our beliefs and experience.
- *Morals* are those values that focus specifically on good and bad. There tends to be more of a social element to morals and a collective, mutual understanding of moral and immoral behavior.
- *Ethics* are externally mandated and accepted guidelines for right and wrong behavior. For example, laws, religion's guidelines such as the Ten Commandments, and specific professional rules for medical doctors or lawyers are all codified sets of ethical behaviors.

To aid in your understanding, think about this dilemma: Is it wrong to steal a loaf of bread to feed your starving family? Your answer will depend on your values, morals, and ethics and the importance you place on each. If your highest value is your family, then you may consider stealing the bread to be good. However, if your highest value is ethics, then you would consider stealing the bread bad. In either case, your intent is irrelevant.

This may appear to be an overly dramatic perspective, and one that does not consider the nuance and considerations that go into the decisions that leaders are forced to make. Sometimes, there is not a good choice, and a leader must choose between two bad options. But these are just excuses. Regardless of them, the most exceptional leaders are those who are ruthlessly ethical.

Unlike values or even morals, ethics by their very nature are in place to establish guidelines for right and wrong behavior. For example, if you are a lawyer, you must not violate attorney-client privilege — you must not repeat what your client tells you in confidence. If you were to break this confidence, you would be acting unethically as a lawyer.

Even if by breaking the confidence you are doing what you feel is morally right, you are still behaving unethically. As a leader, you can't justify unethical behavior because of conflicting morals or values. Violation is violation. We are not implying that you can't make choices as a leader. You can choose to leave the profession of law and no longer be held to the ethical standards of a lawyer. However, you can't have it both ways. This is the binary nature of ethics that exceptional leaders understand and abide by. (It's, therefore, important to make sure your morals do not contradict the ethics of your profession *before* entering the field.)

Obviously, it is very easy to spend excessive energy contemplating the philosophical, metaphysical, and theoretical underpinnings of concepts such as values, morals, and ethics. However, as a practical guide, we recommend avoiding these deep and murky waters. As humans, we have an unbelievable ability to rationalize and justify our actions. Instead of wading in, we recommend that you keep things simple:

Ethics is an established system of right and wrong. As an exceptional leader, your first responsibility is to become knowledgeable about ethical standards that should guide your behavior. After educating yourself on the topic, your responsibility is to ruthlessly adhere to the standards. That's it. No lengthy discourse on how to evaluate and assess your feelings and adherence to the standards. If you find the ethics of the situation contradict your morals, then it's time to leave the situation and find other work. If you don't leave the situation, then you have no room for rationalization or justifying behavior.

In short: just find out what is right and then do it.

INITIATIVE

Initiative is interesting because it is related to both the Action and

Relationships & Character dimensions. Initiative is the catalyst for action—is the inner desire that impels you to take action as a leader. However, we located Initiative within the Relationships & Character dimension because it is the linkage between a leader's initiative and their ability to connect with others interpersonally.

By the very nature of the role, a leader is someone leading the actions of others. What separates an exceptional leader from other leaders is their willingness to roll up their sleeves, get their hands dirty, and do the work themselves. This is the sort of initiative that demonstrates a level of commitment and understanding that followers connect with personally.

Initiative is all about making things happen. We are not implying that the CEO from a Fortune 500 manufacturing company needs to go down to the shop floor and assemble machine parts themselves...but can you imagine if they did? Instead of being sequestered in a suite of executive offices? The imagery of the CEO engaged in helping to make things happen at all levels would be incredibly powerful. This shouldn't be the sort of contrived photo-op that seems to be so popular in helping to establish connections. This should be the sort of authentic experiences that demonstrate a leader's willingness to make things happen.

In the United States, one of the most popular reality television series is called *Undercover Boss*. The series takes corporate executives, changes their appearance, and has them work alongside some of the frontline personnel from their organizations. One of the reasons the show is so powerful are the revelations that executives have about the individuals they are working with—a strong example of the importance of empathy we covered previously. A secondary theme of the show is that it builds on previously non-existent interpersonal connections between bosses and employees. The dynamic works both ways. The leader understands the employees better and the employees feel more connected to the leader.

Our personal experience further confirms this observation. While working as a junior consultant in a large organization, we often had to work six or seven days a week. It was part of the culture and our responsibility to get the work done in support of our clients. Over the years, we observed that we tended to have two types of team leaders:

1. Individuals who, after going through the meat grinder and being promoted, felt entitled to move into more of a hands-off management role—giving direction but choosing not to come in over the weekends even though their team was still expected to do so.
2. Leaders who would not only work any time they expected their team to work, but worked even longer hours when necessary, after they'd sent junior team members home.

Of the two types of leader, which do you think had stronger team morale? Which do you think had consistently higher success rates? Which is the leader you would prefer to follow? The answer is obvious. The leaders who demonstrate initiative through their ability to make things happen are the leaders whom people want to follow. People don't like to be talked at, scolded, or otherwise manipulated. These tricks may work for a short while, but eventually people become aware of the manipulation and become interpersonally disconnected. At this point, there is no leadership in an authentic sense. There may be power, there may be management, but there is not leadership.

To develop your capacity to take initiative, we suggest a very simple exercise. Select one area within your leadership context and get involved at the most fundamental level possible. For example, if you are a team leader whose team must work over a weekend, make sure that you are present. If you lead a team responsible for assembling devices, make sure that you occasionally twist a screw or turn a wrench. If you demonstrate your initiative and proactively solve problems, you will become more accessible and easier to connect with interpersonally.

As an exceptional leader, one of your main responsibilities is to make things happen. You can develop this ability through your initiative and effort. By demonstrating your commitment and ability to proactively solve problems, you will develop stronger and more meaningful interpersonal connections with others that you lead. This reciprocal relationship will help to further reinforce your ability to make things happen now and in the future.

INTEGRITY

Have you ever heard the Will Rogers quote, "It takes a lifetime to build a good reputation, but you can lose it in a minute"? This is a famous quote for good reason: it captures a universal truth. Integrity is one of the entry conditions to being recognized as a leader. If you don't have a good reputation, and if your integrity is constantly in question, you will find it tremendously difficult to be any sort of a leader, let alone an exceptional one.

The good news is that as a leader, and someone who is on a journey to becoming an exceptional leader, you have total control over your integrity. The key to success in building and maintaining your integrity is to keep it simple. After spending decades working with leaders, conducting hundreds of hours of interviews, and reading thousands of journal articles and books, we found the leaders who are consistently the most successful are those who can keep things simple.

In the academic world, we call this a *parsimonious* model. In this context, parsimonious means that all things being equal, the simplest model is best. For example, if something can be described in three words or thirty words, the three-word description is the most parsimonious.

This has been a guiding principle for our work. We could spend a full chapter, or even a full book, unpacking the various nuances and descriptions of integrity. Instead, we've parsed it down to three key elements:

1. You must act with integrity.
2. You must lead by example.
3. You must be willing to take accountability for your actions and those of your organization.

The first element that separates exceptional leaders from everyone else is their commitment to act with integrity. To act with integrity is to be honest and to adhere to one's own strict moral and ethical principles. It is not possible to have integrity and be unethical, dishonest, or immoral. These characteristics are so intertwined that it is almost impossible to see where one ends and the other begins. As a leader, you have a responsibility to act with integrity not only when you know you are being watched, but also when no one is looking.

Imagine you are driving home late at night and the roads are deserted. You come to a four-way stop in your neighborhood and start to slow down. As you slow down, you look left and right, and don't see any headlights and or anyone on the sidewalk. Do you come to a full stop, or do you half-brake and slowly roll through the intersection? Integrity is about coming to a full and complete stop before moving through the intersection. Even though there were no other cars coming, and no one would ever know whether you came to a full stop or not, you would know.

Chances are that if you have ever driven a car you have executed a rolling stop when you were either in a hurry or saw no one was around. We chose this example because it helps to illustrate the sort of rationalizations that even the most ethical and moral of us can make. Any success as a leader obtained without integrity is destined to be short-lived.

As a bonus, when you act with integrity, it is like buying insurance against future regret. Let's return to our stop sign scenario. What if a bicyclist came out from the shadows at the exact moment you rolled through the intersection? Taking the extra split-second to do the right thing might save you a lifetime of remorse. When you act with integrity, both when you know you are being watched as well as when you are not, you naturally begin to embody our second recommendation: leading by example.

When you lead by example, you provide a model for those around you. Integrity must be demonstrated through action, not just words. All the integrity speeches and training in the world are worthless if you as a leader do not have integrity. The phrase, a fish rots from the head down, means failures by an organization are usually a result of leadership failures. It is illogical to expect others to act with integrity if you don't lead by example and act with integrity yourself. When you lead by example, others should naturally pattern themselves off what they see you doing. Our third recommendation specifically addresses how leaders can address integrity challenges.

We have found that exceptional leaders take accountability for their actions and those of their organization. To err is human, and we are not so naïve as to believe that it is possible to go through life without the occasional lapse in judgment. This book provides a practical model for leadership, one that we know can be successful in the real world. As a leader, you will make mistakes. Your team will also make mistakes. Exceptional leaders are those who immediately recognize these transgressions and take steps to resolve the issues and make amends. Sometimes, it may be necessary to take responsibility for the actions of those you lead. These are the burdens that a leader must be willing to bear. If you are unwilling to bear them, you will never be an exceptional leader.

To help cultivate and protect your integrity, we recommend that you first establish your own moral and ethical code. This code should be inclusive of any laws and regulations that you have already identified while establishing your ethical character; however, it should also be more inclusive. You should take the time to contemplate the importance of honesty and that failing to speak up can be a transgression of omission. Integrity is non-negotiable when it comes to being an exceptional leader; your ability to develop trusting and beneficial interpersonal connections and relationships will depend on it. Therefore, our next recommendation is to keep things simple for yourself; just follow your code. When your thoughts and actions are guided by your code, you will act with integrity; when you act with integrity, you lead by example; and when the inevitable mistakes happen, you take accountability for both yourself and your organization.

LIFE-LONG LEARNING

When it comes to cognition and brain function, research has shown time and again that there are only two directions: growth and decline. There is no such thing as a learning plateau where you can stop learning and not experience decline. This is based in human biology.

Take a moment to let this fact resonate. As humans, we are either cognitively growing or cognitively declining; there is no middle ground.

Think of your brain as a muscle. A muscle that is used on a regular basis and when supplied the necessary calories will strengthen. Increase the use, and the muscle grows stronger. Decrease the use, and the muscle weakens and declines. Stop using the muscle entirely, and it atrophies. This is just nature.

We wanted to spend so much time on the underlying law of nature that drives the need for life-long learning, because unless you fully embrace the fundamental need, you will struggle with making it a priority. Life-long learning is more about mindset and perspective than it is about tasks. There is no right way to embody life-long learning, but there must be desire and sustained effort. And once you accept that cognition, or brain function, is binary, either growing or declining, deciding which direction you want to go should be obvious.

In addition to the biological mandate to continue to learn and grow, there are other benefits to sustained learning. We live in exciting times. The pace of change and technology advancements makes it necessary for everyone to constantly learn new tools and approaches. For example, with the advent of smartphones, we can get the news, send emails, make phone calls, check on our friends, take pictures, read books, check on our friends and colleagues…all before we go to work in the morning and all in the palm of our hand. If you don't make it a priority to learn about new technologies, you will become a relic of a past age, someone irrelevant in the new world. The more you can push yourself to learn, the more confident and relevant you will become.

How is life-long learning related to becoming an exceptional leader? The linkage is through the role modeling your behavior has on others, and how this behavior can help build, maintain, and strengthen interpersonal connections.

When you are a leader, your actions are constantly observed. If you demonstrate a commitment to continuous and life-long learning, you will also demonstrate your commitment to improving and becoming an expert. If you want others to put their trust in you as a leader, your commitment to growing your expertise will be paramount. For example, if you go to a new doctor's office and see that all the magazines and medical journals are at least 10 years old, how confident will you be that this individual will be an expert on the most contemporary medical techniques?

When we moved a few years ago, we had to find new doctors. One of the first that we met with appeared to be 150 years old and had magazines from the late 1990s in his waiting room. Although he might have been very competent, there was absolutely no way we were going to allow him to be our medical leader.

As leaders, we don't want to fall into the trap of being perceived as irrelevant by those we are trying to lead. We must push ourselves to remain relevant and contemporary. Otherwise, no one will be willing to follow our lead.

To establish a commitment to life-long learning, and to ensure that you are maximizing your potential to build and cultivate interpersonal connections as a leader, we suggest the following:

1. Demonstrate a broadened perspective on major issues affecting your industry.
2. Demonstrate competence by expanding and improving the knowledge and skills you need to be a leader.
3. Demonstrate life-long learning through continued personal and professional development.

Let's go over these one at a time.

When you demonstrate a broadened perspective on major issues affecting your industry, you are showing your relevance. You don't have to become the definitive authority on every issue, but you must be willing to spend the time and effort to become knowledgeable. For example, if you are in the agricultural industry, you should read publications from commodity groups to learn about trends or potential policy challenges. If you raise cattle, what are some of the critical issues? Are there potential impacts from Environmental Protection Agency mandates? Is the industry lobbying to increase export trade with foreign countries? How will the prices of grain commodities affect feed costs? These are the types of issues that you should have a perspective about.

Next, we have found that exceptional leaders differentiate themselves by showing a commitment to expanding and improving the knowledge and skills necessary to be a competent leader. Congratulations! By reading this book, you are demonstrating your commitment to becoming a more competent leader. You are already well on your way to integrating this recommendation into your life-long learning commitment.

Exceptional leaders are those who recognize that there is not a leadership destination, only a journey. Although we hope this book serves as a tremendous resource, we also hope that you continue to seek other leadership development opportunities. There are many areas where we have only covered the most fundamental information necessary to develop your leadership capacity. Each of us has innate dispositions and interest areas; hopefully, this book has initiated your curiosity about one or more topics.

Finally, life-long learning for the exceptional leader is not restricted to professional development; personal development is also necessary. It is important to strive for balance as a leader. If all your learning and development is limited to specific professional pursuits, you are missing out on a world of other possibilities.

Learning only about professional areas is like going to the gym and only doing bicep curls. Over time, you might develop well defined arms, but your body would be out of balance — with massive arms and puny legs. Any personal trainer will tell you that the healthiest approach is to work different parts of your body at different times. Ideally, you complete a workout focused on one muscle group and then give that group time to rest and recover while you work on a different group. We recommend the same approach for learning as a leader.

Obviously, industry knowledge and leadership development are critical to being a leader; however, exceptional leaders take the added step of developing themselves personally. Personal learning allows us to better appreciate art and beauty and subtlety. It stimulates creativity and helps us make the neural-connections and pathways that are so critical for meaning making as humans. It is the attempt to create cognitive processes whereby you can effectively blend art and science as an exceptional leader. Our primary recommendation is that you find something that you are passionate about where you can focus your learning and development efforts. Your interests should drive your choices—not for practical or utilitarian reasons, but for the sake of curiosity.

MOTIVATION

The fundamental role for a leader is to influence the actions of others to achieve a common goal, and there is probably no characteristic more critical to success than the ability to motivate others. Without the ability to motivate, there is no way to turn your intentions as a leader into the actions of others. No way to work towards that common goal in a productive and meaningful way.

In many ways, leadership is like a car. There are certain things that are absolutely necessary for a car to operate sufficiently, just like there are certain characteristics that are necessary and non-negotiable for leaders to operate sufficiently. For example, a car will still run with flat tires. It might be slow and inefficient, but it will run. A car will still run with dim headlights, a dirty windshield, a heater that doesn't work, doors that don't lock, and uncomfortable seats. These conditions are unpleasant, but the car will operate. It will get from point A to point B, even though the journey might be painful, slow, and frustrating. However, the car will no longer operate if there is no fuel in the tank. If there is no gasoline, there is no go. The car is no longer a car capable of serving its intended purpose; it is a 4,000-pound roadblock.

A leader without the ability to motivate others is like a car with no gasoline. Such leaders have no ability to power the machine and thus become a roadblock and a hazard. For this reason, one of the primary responsibilities of exceptional leaders is to become experts on different motivational approaches and know which to use in what situation.

You wouldn't put unleaded gasoline in a diesel engine, you wouldn't put diesel in a jet engine, and you wouldn't put jet fuel in an unleaded car engine. There are many different types and grades of fuel available, because there are many different engines. The key is to determine which fuel belongs in which engine. As an exceptional leader, you will need to become capable of leading and persuading others by determining which motivational approach is appropriate in each situation.

For simplicity, we will focus on the primary forms of motivation. There are many other types of motivational approaches, and entire books and fields of study dedicated to the concept, but for our purposes, and from a practical perspective, we will focus on three. The three forms of leadership we will cover are like the three types of fuel we referred to earlier: diesel, unleaded gasoline, and jet fuel—or, in our case: avoid, approach, and self-actualization.

Biologically, every sentient being has two primary motives: approach or avoid. This is true of the most basic forms of life all the way through human beings. If a being can sense light, it will generally approach the light. If the same being is in a well-lit area, and there is an area of darkness, the being will generally avoid the dark space.

You have probably heard the phrase "fight or flight." This is another conceptualization of the same underlying concept. When put in a dangerous situation, there are generally two possible outcomes: the fight mechanism is triggered and the approach motive is engaged, or the flight mechanism is triggered and the avoid motive is engaged.

You may have also heard the phrase "use a carrot or a stick." This saying is generally attributed to getting a donkey to perform a task. First the carrot is used to incentivize the behavior by engaging the approach motive; if the carrot is not sufficient, the stick is used to incentivize the behavior by engaging the avoid motive in the form of a swift pop on the rump. The concept of approach or avoid motivation is well known, because it is inherent in our nature as humans and easily observable in the world around us. Both approach and avoid motives are usually triggered by some sort of external force, so both are known as under a larger heading called "extrinsic motivations."

The extrinsic motivation category is associated with reactions more than with reason and thought. These motives are buried deep in our DNA, so they are very effective, very powerful tools for leaders. As a leader, it may be helpful to think about approach and avoid motivation in terms of the different fuel types we referred to previously. Please note, this is not intended to be a scientific manual on fuel types, so we will make generalities. Our apologies to any engineers or scientists reading this book; we readily acknowledge the liberties we are taking.

When crude oil is pumped, it is unusable to power an engine; only through the refinement process can the raw material turn into something useful. Both diesel and unleaded gasoline are refined in a somewhat similar manner and require a somewhat similar amount of effort. For this reason, diesel and unleaded gasoline represent extrinsic motivation. There are similarities, but the two fuels are not interchangeable.

Diesel is generally used to power big, heavy, slow moving machinery. Similarly, avoid motivation can be a very effective approach. There are times when you must be willing to enforce consequences for actions or behaviors. These are certain situations where non-compliance is not an acceptable outcome. For example, if a surgeon had a patient on the table and asked for a scalpel, the expectation would be that the surgical nurse assisting with the procedure handed over a scalpel without delay or questioning. If the nurse was unwilling or unable to provide the necessary support, they are a liability and should be replaced without delay.

The want to avoid losing one's job, responsibilities, benefits, or standing can be a tremendous motivator.

Because of the potential impacts to interpersonal relationships and the psyches of those you are trying to lead, we recommend that you only use this motivational approach when absolutely necessary. Used in excess, avoid motivation results in being viewed as a tyrant and can severely limit your ability to establish interpersonal connections and excel as a leader. However, to discount the power and appropriateness of this approach under certain conditions is also limiting. We recommend you take the time to think about situations when you might need to use avoid motivation, and how you will ensure you use it appropriately.

Unleaded gasoline is ubiquitous, powering everything from the smallest two-stroke lawn equipment to large passenger vehicles. Similarly, approach motivation is one of the most commonly used methods, and it works in almost all situations.

Leaders have found that others can be motivated by activating desires. For example, a bonus on a paycheck for high-quality work is just money, but what the money represents is a new car or a fancy vacation. A leader does not need to know others' desires; they only need to know how to get certain behaviors by activating those desires.

Approach motivation is a very powerful tool that exceptional leaders know how to engage under the right conditions. Think about the medical example above. What if the Chief of Surgery wanted to encourage their surgical teams to have an even greater level of attention to detail? They could choose to put a policy in place that any mistakes would result in immediate termination, engaging avoid motivation. Or they could put a policy in place where any surgical teams that had 100% error-free surgeries for a period of six-months would receive a bonus equivalent to one-year's salary. The second approach would activate the approach motive and would probably have a much different effect. Take a moment to think about how you might use approach motivation under different situations.

Unlike avoid motivation, overuse of approach motivation will not result in you being considered a tyrant; instead, overuse may result in you being considered a pushover. Approach motivation can be very beneficial and useful, but when it is the only approach you use, where are the consequences when people are not doing what they need to do? Similarly, what do you do if you don't have something that is sufficiently desirable to offer as an award? What if someone is not motivated by money or recognition? How do you keep them engaged and sufficiently motivated? That's where avoid motivation comes in.

To the best of our scientific knowledge, humans are the only species that can engage in self-actualized thought. Meaning, we are the only species that has the capacity to sit and ponder our existence and our place within the vastness of the universe. If approach and avoid motivation are diesel and unleaded gasoline, self-actualized motivation is jet fuel. The level of refinement and potential between diesel and jet fuel is not simply moving one stair higher on the stairway of possibility; it is leaving the diesel behind in the basement and taking an express elevator to the penthouse with jet fuel.

Motivation that occurs at the level of thought and self-perception is known as intrinsic motivation, because it originates from within. Whereas avoid and approach motivations deal with what individuals do or don't want to happen, intrinsic motivation is what an individual wants to be.

This can be one of the most powerful forms of motivation because it taps into some of the most fundamental questions: What is the meaning of life? Who am I? What am I meant to do? These are the questions that drive humans to join together to accomplish feats larger than what any one person would ever be capable of accomplishing alone.

Rockets to outer space, a telecommunications network that can connect almost any two people on the entire planet, food production that has increased on less arable land to feed a global population that has more than quadrupled since 1900. These are not accomplishments possible by making others fearful or trying to induce them into desired behaviors; these are accomplishments possible because individuals saw how their efforts contributed to something larger than themselves. Exceptional leaders know that one of the most powerful motivational approaches is to help others see how they can connect to something larger, and in so doing, allow them to find fulfillment, contentment, and satisfaction.

Referring again to our medical example: instead of threatening to fire individuals for mistakes or giving them huge bonuses for perfection, one could ensure each member of every surgical team was personally connected to the work and the outcomes of their efforts. Each individual's purpose would be to help every single patient have the best possible chance at a successful recovery, better health, and a more fulfilling life. Perfection would not be a desired outcome because it would be rewarded; perfection would be a desired outcome because every team member understood they had a critical role and purpose to fulfill.

When used properly, intrinsic motivation is one of the most powerful tools an exceptional leader can engage. Think about the leaders who have made the largest impact on you. Chances are these individuals helped you to overcome some of your selfish motives and see how you had the potential to connect to a higher purpose. However, just like with extrinsic motivation, there are times when intrinsic motivation may not be appropriate. For example, consider situations where specific rules or protocols need to be followed under emergency conditions. It is more important to have the urgent situation dealt with correctly than to ensure everyone sees the higher purpose in their actions at the time. There is also a risk that if, as a leader, you only use intrinsic motivational tools, you will be considered detached and too abstract.

To help develop your motivational capacity, we recommend you start by focusing on becoming comfortable with the three primary approaches and the situations when they are most effective. Both avoid and approach motivation can be very beneficial when trying to ensure things are done a specific way. Intrinsic motivation is very beneficial when you need to elevate the thought process in support of the desired behavior. Think about situations where you could have used one of these approaches in the past as well as when you will use them in the future. The more comfortable and confident you are in selecting the appropriate motivational fuel, the more exceptional you will be as a leader.

SELF-AWARENESS

Throughout recorded history, one of the most frequent themes is the call for everyone to *know thyself*. Whether it was Plato or the ancient Egyptians or Lao Tzu who first called for this self-awareness is irrelevant. What is important is to recognize the undeniable power of the appeal. Our research has found that exceptional leaders are those who are willing to take an unbiased view of themselves so they can honestly and authentically build their leadership capacities.

Self-awareness gives you the ability to own your position in situations and to better understand your reactions and thought processes. It is not about becoming your own worst critic or being endlessly unsatisfied. Instead, the type of self-awareness we recommend is non-judgmental. The point is not to see what you are doing wrong, but to establish a true and authentic appraisal of yourself as a leader. If you can't be honest with yourself, your journey to becoming an exceptional leader will be slow and potentially blocked.

Typically, when we make this suggestion to leaders we are working with, the response is a confident "I know who I am." Sometimes the statement might even be true, but more frequently the self-awareness that we are suggesting exceeds what humans are able to do without very dedicated effort. Take a moment to answer some of these questions. What is your current or desired leadership role? What impacts do you want to have in this role? What must you accomplish to make these impacts? Are there any barriers preventing you from making these impacts? Are there any barriers that are preventing you from starting the process? Do you have the support necessary to be successful? Do you have the skill and capacities necessary to be successful? This is just a short example list of questions that your self-awareness efforts should cover.

You will also need to authentically reflect on some of your other characteristics. Do you know your personality type or your goal orientation/motive disposition? What is your problem solving, critical thinking, or conflict management style? What is your educational and familial background? These areas will be important for you to assess and be aware of. The more you can compartmentalize yourself in leadership situations, the more you will be able to act authentically and appropriately.

There are three primary areas that we have found exceptional leaders differentiate themselves from everyone else. Exceptional leaders:

1. Continually evaluate their performance.
2. Know their strengths and weaknesses.
3. Seek wisdom through reflection.

There are many other potential areas where self-awareness can be developed and considered; however, these three are the most critical. Let's go over them in more detail.

The first area where exceptional leaders cultivate their self-awareness is in continuously evaluating their self-performance. When we refer to evaluating in this context, we are specifically referring to an unbiased review of actions, behaviors, and outcomes. This evaluation process can manifest in many ways. As you become more comfortable with this process, it is very likely that the areas you will want to evaluate and focus on will change and evolve.

When leaders start evaluating their self-performance, we recommend they begin with three questions:

1. Do I have the technical skills, knowledge, and capacities to be successful?
2. Am I fulfilling my role as a leader by effectively engaging, supporting, and providing direction to those whom I am trying to lead?
3. Am I spending an appropriate amount of time thinking about how to address current and potential challenges?

We suggest that you spend 10 minutes at the end of each day to quickly but authentically answer these questions.

As you become more comfortable with this process, and it becomes integrated into your daily routine, you will want to modify the questions that you are using to evaluate your self-performance. There will likely be situations that you do not handle in the best way possible. We suggest focusing on questions such as, *How do I want to handle situations like this when I experience them in the future?* rather than, *Why did I screw up?* Instead of focusing on the negative aspects of the results, it is more valuable to evaluate the situation objectively and assess what you did well and what could be improved.

The second primary characteristic of exceptional leaders is knowledge and awareness of personal strengths and weaknesses. We all have certain talents that we have either been born with or have developed through effort. We are generally aware of these strengths and tend to feel more comfortable as leaders when we are using them.

However, sometimes we have a strength that is so inherent in our nature that we don't appreciate it as a strength. For example, you might be a natural people person. Talking to others and making new friends is something so natural that it doesn't feel like it takes effort. Because it is not work for you, you may not fully appreciate that interacting with other people can feel like an incredible chore for other people. Even if something comes naturally, you should still acknowledge and appreciate it as a strength.

On the other end of the spectrum, there are weaknesses that every one of us, no matter how hard we work, will have. For many leaders, this is one of the most challenging aspects to the process: recognizing and admitting their weaknesses. Perfection as a leader is an illusion. We all have areas that we need to work on. Perhaps we talk too much during meetings or don't talk enough. Either we have a very dominant presence or are not noticed. The only way that we can improve is by acknowledging the reality of our situation and then taking the steps necessary to develop solutions.

Leaders who are honest and transparent and acknowledge their strengths and weaknesses are the most successful. For example, appreciating weaknesses has been shown to result in stronger interpersonal connections with others.

The final way exceptional leaders develop self-awareness is though reflection. Whereas evaluating your self-performance and knowing your strengths and weaknesses may be academic exercises that you can undertake through routine and discipline, the only way you will ever change is through reflection. You may go through the process of evaluating your daily performance as a leader and may note what happened and how you handled the situation, but if that is where you end the process, you are missing the point. You must take the evaluation observations, couple them with what you know about your personal strengths and weaknesses, and critically reflect on how the two are related and what your intention is for acting in the future. Reflection is the key to synthesizing what you know and turning it into something actionable.

When Socrates said, "The unexamined life is not worth living," we know he was not talking about leadership in the contemporary sense. However, his words are as true and meaningful today as they were in ancient Greece, and they are particularly relevant to anyone who wants to be an exceptional leader. You must become self-aware of your behavior, skills, and areas for improvement.

The more clarity you have about your current condition, the more likely you will be to successfully reach your desired goal. We suggest you start simply: spend 10 minutes a day evaluating and reflecting on your leadership. Through this process, you will become knowledgeable about your strengths and weaknesses. The more you are aware of your strengths and weaknesses, the more productive your evaluation and reflections will be. The more energy you commit to this virtuous cycle, the more expedient your journey to becoming an exceptional leader.

UNDERSTANDING AND APPRECIATING DIVERSITY

To address the challenges in their world, the very earliest humans relied on stone tools. Whether they were smooth stones for grinding grains or sharpened arrowheads for hunting game, the stone tools were an adaptation to the environment. As hunting and gathering gave way to more permanent settlements and cultivated agriculture, the sophistication of tools increased dramatically. Instead of blunted axe heads made of chipped stone, there was a need for sharp instruments capable of reaping and other tasks.

The necessity for more complex tools led to the consideration of other source materials to create the tools. Metal was naturally occurring and relatively easy to locate. Moving from stone to copper tools represented a paradigm shift for early humans. Now humans had a means to create what they needed without being completely dependent on what they could find in nature. Copper tools were limited only by the ability to find enough copper, melt it, and fill the desired tool mold.

However, copper tools had a major limitation: they were incredibly flimsy. Compared with stones that were rigid but brittle, the copper tools were durable but pliable. Tools that constantly bent or quickly became dull were not ideal. An ideal tool was one that combined the long-lasting sharpness and rigidity of stone tools with the durability and utility of copper tools. In the pursuit of a more ideal tool, someone had the inspiration to combine multiple metals together to see if the result would have improved qualities and characteristics.

One such combination was copper and tin. Independently, both metals are malleable and lack robust characteristics; however, when combined, something exceptional happens. The two metals become something greater and more powerful than their constituent parts—and so the Bronze Age was born. Humans shifted from nomadic to permanent settlements. They had the ability to cultivate crops as well as politics, art, science, humanities, and all the other studies we enjoy today.

Obviously, this book is not intended to be a history text, so the previous summary has been simplified dramatically. Nevertheless, our intent was to demonstrate the awesome power that can result from combining diverse elements. As leaders, we may not be working with metals, but we are working with an even more precious set of elements: the insights, perspectives, wisdom, and talents of those we work with.

Exceptional leaders are those who understand and appreciate diversity and know the power and value that can result when applied intentionally. As a leader, you will be responsible for cultivating an appreciation of different perspectives and opinions as well as an openness to differences. It is the complementary characteristics of copper and tin that result in bronze; similarly, it is the diverse but complementary perspectives of different people that make for the most robust group dynamic.

We have found that there are two main areas where exceptional leaders distinguish themselves in their understanding and appreciation of diversity. Exceptional leaders:

1. Act inclusively.
2. Are adaptable and collaborative and can work with diversity.

You have probably heard the saying, "Birds of a feather flock together." There is a natural tendency to surround ourselves with others who share similar characteristics, such as nationality, race and ethnicity, gender, age, religious beliefs, level of education, socio-economic status, and many other types of group identification. Exceptional leaders are those who can transcend these barriers and intentionally act inclusively with others.

To determine whether you are acting inclusively with others, we recommend you ask yourself the following questions:

- Does everyone on your team share the same general characteristics and approaches to problem solving?
- Have you as a leader specifically engaged those with differing points of view?

- Do your words and actions align when it comes to appreciating diversity?

As you answer these questions, we suggest you think of ways you can act more inclusively. For example, if you find your team shares many of the same characteristics, how can you infuse more diversity into the group? Next, as you encourage more diversity, how will you as the leader ensure that a safe space is provided to encourage diverse points of view? Finally, what can you do to exemplify the type of behavior you wish to cultivate?

As you consider these questions, you should set specific goals for yourself. Perhaps you want to make sure that everyone on your team has a chance to speak during meetings. The key is for you to set reasonable goals for yourself and then work towards those goals through ongoing tracking and reflection. The first step is to become aware of the need and then ensure you are acting inclusively.

The second area where exceptional leaders differentiate themselves is through their adaptability and collaborative work with diversity. As a leader, there may be times when you need to appreciate that your perspective may not be consistent with others. Exceptional leaders are those who can acknowledge their position in a situation and make decisions accordingly.

One of the most fascinating and challenging aspects of working with leaders from around the globe is acknowledging our differences while not trying to impose our perspectives as the only answer. For example, while working on a large consulting project in the early 2000s, it was necessary for us to travel to India and spend several months working with a local team to set up a new center. Going from rural Colorado to Bangalore, India was culture shock. The first two weeks were an extremely frustrating time. The sights, sounds, and smells were almost overwhelming. Likewise, the team, while incredibly talented and eager, was very different from teams in the United States.

There were many differences in the team versus others we had worked with. For example, the perception of deadlines and the expected distance between the team and leaders was astounding. However, after the first couple of weeks of immersion, we had a huge epiphany: it was not their responsibility to adapt to us; it was our responsibility as leaders to adapt and collaborate to the diverse environment we were in.

Being an exceptional leader is not always about being right or getting your way. Instead, leaders who can demonstrate adaptability and the ability to collaborate with diversity are those who consistently produce the highest quality, most valuable results. We recommend you think about a time when you had to work with diversity. It does not have to be a work-related situation; perhaps you went to party and found you were the only person who liked a certain genre of music or sports team. How did you react in this situation? Were you adaptable? Were you willing to collaborate for the benefit of the group?

It is important to have a perspective as a leader; that is the nature of the role. However, exceptional leaders are those who look for opportunities to include others, as well as demonstrate their adaptability and ability to collaborate. Remember the shift that occurred when copper and tin were combined to make bronze? The complementary diversity of the elements created something even greater than the constituent parts. As a leader, the more you can understand and appreciate diversity, the more you can harness its awesome power to create exceptional results.

SUMMARY

Connecting with others interpersonally is one of the defining characteristics of an exceptional leader. It is what separates power from leadership. With enough power, almost anyone can manipulate others; however, that is not the same as leadership. If you rely only on power, then when you lose that power, so too will you lose the willingness of others to act. By contrast, leadership is rooted not in a power base but in interpersonal connections that impel and inspire others to act.

We have worked with many technically capable people who were unsuccessful moving into leadership roles. One of the main reasons for these failures was an inability to connect personally and cultivate the interpersonal connections necessary for success. However, when these individuals were made aware of shifts necessary to be successful in their new roles, and when they actively worked to develop these traits and characteristics, each one of them experienced an increase in leadership capacity. We have complete confidence that you will have the same experience.

In this chapter, we covered nine critical relationship and character traits of exceptional leaders. We provided definitions and recommendations for developing confidence, empathy, ethics, initiative, integrity, life-long learning, motivation, self-awareness, and an understanding and appreciation for diversity. These areas are all necessary. The good news is these traits and characteristics are completely within your control. There is nothing on this list that you can't develop by using intentional effort. When you accept the responsibility for these traits and characteristics, you will be prepared to create strong interpersonal connections with others and perform as an exceptional leader.

The next chapter addresses strategic planning, an area central to what constitutes a leader. We will identify what the most exceptional leaders do as well as how to develop these areas for yourself.

STRATEGIC PLANNING

It is not enough to be busy. So are the ants. The question is: What are we busy about?

—*Henry David Thoreau*

Leaders are, by definition, those individuals who influence others in pursuit of a common goal. At the most fundamental level, the common goal is the reason why leaders must have the capacity to strategically plan. Strategic planning is also the ability to think critically and provide a vision. On your journey to becoming an exceptional leader, you must accept the necessity of the connection between strategic planning and a common goal. Without one, there is no need for the other. Without either, there is no need for leadership.

The importance of this connection is evidenced by the multiple leadership models that focus solely on it. We agree: leaders must be competent in strategic planning if they wish to be successful. Depending on your leadership role, you may not believe that you have much influence on strategic planning. We would contend that all leaders have a role to play when it comes to strategic planning. The scope of influence might be different from leader to leader; however, the connection to a common goal is equally important.

Strategic planning tends to have an air of mystique around it, as though it were an area of specialization for only the most exceptional business consultants. Our experience is that this prestige is generally a mirage, a well-developed formula these consultants use to command astronomical fees. We have found the competencies necessary to be successful in strategic planning as a leader can be developed by anyone. However, before you can effectively develop these competencies, you must believe that you can.

If you have any doubts or hesitation about your ability to be successful in strategic planning, we offer up this quote from Walt Disney: "I only hope that we don't lose sight of one thing—that it was all started by a mouse."

> *There is nothing that is impossible if you have the strength to begin and the fortitude to continue.*

You will experience inevitable setbacks and frustrations. There may be areas that come very naturally and others that require immense personal effort to overcome. However, if you believe, and if you nurture that belief, you can develop your ability to strategically plan. As a result, you will be that much further on your journey to becoming an exceptional leader.

In this chapter, we will cover the six different strategic planning dimensions of exceptional leaders: critical thinking, decision making, global and systems thinking, goal setting and visioning, problem solving, and stakeholder assessment. Remember, strategic planning is about the common goal you are trying to achieve. The more effectively you as a leader help others move towards that goal, the more successful your results.

CRITICAL THINKING

As a leader, one of your most important responsibilities will be to acquire and process information to help provide direction to others. This is and will continue to be a vital role for leaders as the numbers of data and information sources available grow every day. Without the proper tools and capabilities, this amount of information can cause overload. The saying, attempting to drink from the firehose, is appropriate. Although the information we want and need is available, it is so overwhelming that it is not very useful.

One of the most effective tools available to collect, comprehend, and act upon information necessary to support strategic planning is critical thinking. The popularity of critical thinking as a concept in both education and business is a strong indicator of the power of this skill. Like for most terms, there are many different definitions and interpretations of critical thinking. As it relates to exceptional leadership, we define critical thinking as the ability of an individual to process information in an appropriate manner to form a judgment.

We use this definition based on our research in critical thinking. Just like for leadership, there are many different models and theories about critical thinking. Some theories propose critical thinking is a natural disposition, like intelligence or personality. In these models, critical thinking tends to range from low to high. Other theories suggest critical thinking is a skill that can be learned, much like reading or math. No one is born with the ability to read, but through dedicated training and effort, one can learn. These models indicate that there is a correct way to think critically that can be taught and followed.

Our critical thinking model is a synthesis of these two primary theories. Because critical thinking is a cognitive process, it is absolutely related to our biology as individuals. Just as you have a natural disposition towards introversion or extroversion, you also have a natural critical thinking style. What we disagree with is the notion that an individual's critical thinking approach can be measured on some definitive ranking scale. Any sort of standardized scale that attempts to quantify critical thinking in this way is helpful only under very specific conditions — and often these quantified attempts do more harm than good.

We have found there is a continuum for critical thinking styles, and that as an individual you will have a certain disposition. Our continuum is judgment-free and provides a starting point for understanding your natural inclinations. Specifically, we have found that individuals range from critical thinking *engagers* to critical thinking *seekers*.

Engagers think critically by examining new information relative to their existing knowledge base. Seekers think critically by seeking out new information unrelated to their current knowledge base. You can find more information about our tool, the University of Florida Critical Thinking Inventory (UFCTI), online. For the purposes of supporting your journey to becoming an exceptional leader, the most important thing for you is to acknowledge that critical thinking is a personal process, and that there is no such thing as context-free high or low critical thinking.

You have all the tools necessary to be an exceptional critical thinker.

The second main theory base indicates that critical thinking can be taught, typically in a very specific way. We agree with the perspective that critical thinking can be taught. Our research and personal experience affirm this fact. However, we don't agree that critical thinking is something that needs to be done in a rigid manner following a prescribed procedure. Leadership, and really anything having to do with humans, is an incredibly messy affair. Real life does not function like school textbooks full of contrived questions with right or wrong answers. We have found that exceptional leaders are those who are aware of their natural critical thinking disposition and use a flexible approach to critical thinking because they know that not every problem can be solved used the same procedure.

One way to think about this approach is to consider the difference between a concert band and a jazz band. In both cases, musicians have to pick instruments to play (natural disposition), then learn the fundamentals of the instruments (training). However, at a certain level of proficiency, there is a distinction between the two modes. The individual who plays in a concert follows carefully directed sheet music, whereas the jazz musician riffs and plays off the themes and moods of their fellow band members.

Exceptional leaders are more like jazz musicians when it comes to critical thinking. They are aware of their natural disposition and have learned the necessary skills to be successful. They then use these skills flexibly and creatively as the situation dictates. For this reason, we recommend developing the underlying skills necessary to be successful, but then using those skills to process information in an appropriate manner. There are four specific skills that exceptional leaders use to think critically. Exceptional leaders:

1. Seek out multiple views and take an overview of the information.
2. Integrate multiple perspectives and systems.
3. Ask appropriate questions and reflect on the answers.
4. Challenge existing ways of thinking.

First, when exceptional leaders seek out multiple views, they make sure they have the right information to make the best decision possible. Limited information leads to limited results. As a leader, it is your responsibility to connect to the data sources that are most relevant to what you want to accomplish. We recommend you start with at least three different information sources when you are seeking multiple views. For example, if you want to know what your organization is doing well and what needs to be improved, you may start with an internal perspective. Asking your team their thoughts would be very helpful. Next, you may want to get an external perspective, such as your customers' insights. Finally, you may want to look for an objective information source; benchmarking your results with peer organizations would be a good way to see how you are doing. Collecting multiple views will help you develop an overview of the situation.

Second, after collecting the necessary information, exceptional leaders integrate multiple perspectives and systems. Continuing with our organizational assessment example, the three sets of information will need to be analyzed, evaluated, and integrated. What are the consistencies between all three sources? What are the differences? Themes or trends should be identified. The key is to be able to take information and consolidate it and integrate it into something more usable.

After the information is as integrated as possible, exceptional leaders ask appropriate questions and reflect on the answers. If the external and objective information is consistent but the internal results are drastically different, this is a flag for following up with additional questions. Why would internal respondents have such a different view? Are there specific areas or items that might be responsible for the difference? Are there any other results that were inconsistent with what you thought they would be? If yes, what are they?

Do the results indicate that you need to change your perspective? The key to effective critical thinking is to *think*. Ask questions about the information and don't just accept it as is. We recommend you start with a set of generic questions like the ones we've proposed. The more you get comfortable with the approach and intent, the more you can adjust and modify the questions to suit your personal style. The goal is to develop the skills and empower you to use them as appropriate.

Finally, exceptional leaders challenge existing ways of thinking. As a leader, you must have the fortitude to periodically defy conventional thinking and ways of doing things. We are not suggesting that to be an exceptional leader you must become a gadfly constantly challenging the norm; however, you must be willing to periodically ask the tough questions. Why is something done the way that it is? Can we remove steps from this process? Is this activity necessary anymore? The more you can challenge existing ways of thinking in an appropriate manner, the more effective you will be as a leader.

Critical thinking can be a tremendous tool for leaders. Once you recognize your natural dispositions towards critical thinking and build a basic set of skills, you can cultivate your own personal approach. Exceptional leaders are those who can process information critically and create meaning and insights. As a result, they are more effective at strategic planning and helping guide their teams to common goals.

DECISION MAKING

As a leader, you will have an almost unlimited exposure to both information and possibilities. Exceptional leaders are those who can gather enough information to make a decision and then act decisively. Deciding is a form of action, and all action is a consequence of choice. If you decide, you are choosing to act. If you fail to decide, you are choosing not to act.

When we are young, we are encouraged to try new things. There are no expectations for perfection. In fact, failure is accepted as a precondition for success. If the expectation was perfection, no one would ever learn to walk. If the first time you tried to take a step, you were overwhelmed with self-doubt and concerns that you would not be successful, you might not ever have had the willpower to attempt the step.

Thankfully, this is not how we are wired as humans. We don't come preloaded with doubts, fears, and hesitation—we keep things simple.

It is for this reason that we have repeatedly encouraged you to keep things simple as a leader. Through the process of growing up, we lose the simplicity with which we are born. We become judgmental of ourselves and concerned with how others see us. We learn the consequences of our actions and feel the pain associated with failure. The reason for this shift is hidden deep within our biology and is a consequence of our most basic motives—approach or avoid.

When we are young, we receive praise and recognition for not only our actions, but also our attempts. The toddler learning how to walk is given constant reinforcement and praise and so feels the satisfaction of approach motivation. Over time, we begin to fear failure because we associate it with punishment. As we grow up and move through the educational system, our desire to avoid punishment becomes a very strong motivation. For example, if you did not explicitly follow the direction for writing a paper but instead used a more creative approach and subsequently received a failing grade, you are not likely to make another creative attempt. It is more desirable to not be punished than to try something new.

This is an unfortunate cycle that becomes very limiting as we mature and especially when we take on leadership roles. Exceptional leaders are those who recognize failure precedes success; therefore, they can act decisively and decide without being paralyzed with fear that their decision is incorrect. Failure is not something that should be punished; it should be valued as a learning and growth opportunity. When we are not successful, it is not punishment from the outside that is the most damaging, but the way we punish ourselves.

All leaders, no matter how confident or self-assured, have doubts. We have worked with thousands of leaders from some of the largest and most successful organizations in the world. Every single one of them has moments of self-doubt. It is not the absence of doubt that separates exceptional leaders from everyone else; it is the ability to manage those doubts and make decisions accordingly. When decisions end up in failure, these leaders learn important lessons and try to identify what can be done differently in the future. They don't over-analyze results.

Here is a simple and effective approach. To start, think about your decision-making process. Are you decisive, or does it feel like you never have enough information to make the right choice? When you make a decision, do you proceed with confidence or repeatedly questions whether it was the right move? When decisions you make end up with undesirable results, do you think about what you did wrong, or do you think about what you should do differently next time? There should not be any judgment associated with this analysis, but if you are not honest about where you are today, you will find it very difficult to change.

Once you have an honest assessment of how you approach decision-making today, take some time to watch a toddler learning how to walk. If you don't have easy access to a toddler, you can watch a video on YouTube. As you watch the first steps, notice the pattern. There is the belief that walking can be accomplished. There is the attempt. There is inevitable failure that results in a fall back to the ground. Watch what happens next. In almost every case, the toddler laughs and then works to get up and take another attempt.

Kids are amazing in this way, because they have not been burdened with the self-doubt and fears that we accumulate as we grow up. They haven't yet developed a full range of emotions and cognition; instead, they represent our most fundamental selves as humans. We are naturally willing to make decisions. We are naturally willing to accept failure as a pre-condition of success. We don't naturally beat ourselves up over failure; instead, we get up and try again. This is the simplicity that exceptional leaders use when it comes to decision making.

How can you better embody these characteristics in your decision-making process? Are you uncomfortable or unable to make decisions because you are afraid to fail? If so, we recommend you reorient your perspective to see failures as rungs on the ladder to eventual success. These are not setbacks; these are experiences that are taking you one step closer to where you want to be.

If you struggle with not being able to make a decision because you don't feel like you have all the information necessary, we encourage you to accept the reality that you will never have all the information. Don't allow yourself to go into analysis paralysis; a good decision today is more desirable than a perfect decision tomorrow. Keep your analysis and information-gathering simple. When you get mired in minutia, decision making becomes more difficult.

Leadership is all about helping direct others towards a common goal. The goal is the desired destination for the group. As a leader, it is your responsibility to provide a map of how to move from the current location to the destination. Exceptional leaders are those who recognize decision making as fundamental to their responsibility to provide a strategic plan and help their team arrive at the desired destination.

GLOBAL AND SYSTEMS THINKING

There may have been a time when a leader could specialize in a specific area, focus all their efforts in that area, ignore almost everything else, and still be successful. This is no longer the case. The world is too interconnected, the pace is too fast, and the expectations are too high. Leaders today must think in terms of both the big picture and their specialization—think globally and act locally. They understand and appreciate their efforts do not happen in a vacuum and that systems thinking demands they focus on the whole rather than the parts.

Chances are you engage in systems thinking whether you are aware of it or not. Systems thinking requires that you look at both events and the longer view. Think about a time when you were driving and noticed that your fuel tank was almost empty. What was your response? There were probably a couple of thoughts that came to mind. *How far can I drive before I am totally out of fuel? Is this an emergency, or do I have some flexibility?* If you have some flexibility, you might next think about what you need to accomplish while in your car. *How far away is my destination? Can I reach my destination based on the amount of fuel I have remaining?* If your destination is very close, you might not have any problems; if your destination is far away, you will definitely need to fill up. *What is the event at the destination? Is there a specific time I need to arrive?* If there is a specific deadline, what are the consequences if you are late? If you are a few minutes late because you stop for fuel, will that be all right? If you run out of fuel and miss the appointment all together, what are the consequences? If this is a job interview for which being late is not a viable option, then risking running out of fuel to arrive on time might be worth it.

This micro-situation is that sort of systems thinking that we are recommending. Exceptional leaders see the connection between things, not just the things themselves. The fuel gauge is an event; the interconnection between what the fuel gauge represents and what you are attempting to accomplish is what is important. The fuel gauge is connected to the fuel in your vehicle, which is connected to the distance to your destination, which is connected to the time sensitivity of your destination, which is connected to the importance you associate with the activity.

The goal of systems thinking is to see things in a more integrated and less fragmented way. It is very important to keep this simple goal at the forefront of your thinking as we describe how exceptional leaders use systems thinking to improve their strategic planning capacity.

We have found that exceptional leaders consider situations from social, cultural, economic, political, and environmental perspectives. The connections between these five perspectives provide a complete picture for these leaders and give them tremendous insight. Approaching situations in a pragmatic way gives these leaders the ability to see around corners, predict potential issues, and make sure to plan and address potential roadblocks.

How can anyone possibly have the time to think about all these connections in all situations? The answer is to keep it simple, develop a pattern, and then continue to work on improving. (This should be a familiar method by now.)

Previously, we worked with one of the largest consumer goods manufacturers in the world. It had hundreds of brands and made everything from toothpaste to condiments to laundry detergent to shampoo. The company was interested in improving the effectiveness of its training delivery around the globe, which included over 70 different countries. We helped to create a system for tracking the training that was going on around the globe and centralized the vendor management and payment operations. It was a huge initiative.

We used the five system thinking perspectives to develop an approach that was well received and cost effective:

1. *Social implications.* In the past, business unit leads managed all the vendor relationships themselves; we had to make sure the relationships would not be impacted by our changes.
2. *Cultural considerations.* For a large corporate client, this included two layers of consideration: the corporate culture and the different country cultures. We had to make sure we were developing communications that were culturally sensitive to minimize misunderstandings and pushback.
3. *Economic impacts.* The company, business units, and vendors all

had to see the benefit to the change.
4. *Political ramifications.* Some countries had very strong union presences with significant political influence. We had to proactively manage these relationships while staying informed about the political climate of each country.
5. *Environmental impacts.* In this situation, the change was more administrative than physical, so the environmental impacts would be minimal. Through the centralized platform, we could source vendors more effectively, reducing the amount of travel required to deliver services. The reduced travel had a positive impact on the environment, even though that was not necessarily an intended outcome.

Despite being simplified dramatically, this example demonstrates how we recommend you begin thinking about situations and issues you face as a leader. We are confident that the more you use a systems thinking approach, the more natural it will become. We also recommend you practice using a systems thinking approach for other issues that may not be within your area of control but may have an impact on your efforts as a leader. What are the main issues that are facing your industry? What local, regional, national, or global issues might have an impact? What are the social, cultural, economic, political, and environmental connections between these issues? Issues can range from workforce preparation, to taxes, to licensing, to regulations and policy, and to severe weather events. These are huge global issues that could have a dramatic impact on your ability to lead. Exceptional leaders are those who demonstrate an ability to engage in systems thinking and use this approach to inform and improve their strategic planning.

GOAL SETTING AND VISIONING

Leaders set goals. This is not an earth-shaking revelation, because it is consistent with what a leader fundamentally does. A leader influences a group of other individuals to achieve a common goal. Without a goal—some desired end or destination—there is not much need for leadership. We have found exceptional leaders are those who link goal setting with visioning. Goal setting and visioning are not independent so much as they are interdependent. Exceptional leaders recognize that a goal is necessary but insufficient. Only when the goal is combined with a vivid, well-described, easily understood, and supportable vision of the desired goal or end state can leadership magic happen.

Goal setting and visioning is another area where the distinction between leadership and personal development can become blurred. From a personal development perspective, goal setting is very important because it serves as a guide for personal actions and choices. For example, a personal goal might be to run at least five miles per week for the next month. This may be a great goal, but it is not the sort of goal we are referring to within a leadership context. A leadership goal might be to increase your team profit margin by 10% over the next year. A leadership goal must include a shared vision for the desired outcome. Everyone on the team must be able to understand how they can contribute to the goal and support the outcome. A personal goal is completely dependent upon the goal setter. While a vision for the desired end state might be helpful, it is only applicable to the person setting the goal. There is no opportunity for shared vision.

How do exceptional leaders go about setting goals and visioning? Think about the last leadership goal you set. If you can't think of a past leadership-related goal, think of a goal that you would like to set. What are the characteristics of the goal? Did you have a clear idea of what it would look like when you achieved the goal? How would you know you were making progress towards the goal? Was there buy-in from everyone involved in pursuing the goal? Was the goal realistic? Did you know when you wanted to achieve the goal? Did you clearly describe why the goal was important?

Anyone who has been exposed to leadership or personal development knows that goal setting is important, so we are always amazed at how few leaders take the time to set goals correctly. There are generally three categories of leaders when it comes to goal setting:

1. Leaders whose goals are dictated by some outside force. If these individuals are in a corporate setting, these might be departmental goals handed down from above. There is very little buy-in and generally no vision because the goal is more like a decree: "This must be done."
2. Leaders who use the strong-start, poor execution approach to goal setting. In this scenario, the leader has an idea for the goal and takes some time to think and plan about how to proceed. There is a vision for the desired end-state that is shared at the beginning of the process. The strong start is commendable; however, inevitably circumstances change, and the goal gets forgotten. In some cases, words and actions start to run contrary to the stated goal. We once worked with an organization that had a goal to provide superior customer service to differentiate themselves from their competitors. The economy then took a downturn, and the organization decided that one of the easiest places to save money was in its customer service department, so it promptly laid off 20% of that workforce. This was not a strategic reduction of staff to improve quality by removing poor performers; this was a pure cost-savings measure, and they lost many fantastic customer service reps. You can't grow through cuts. In subsequent years, the organization

struggled because its customer service was no longer superior; it was average at best. Additionally, the company's credibility and integrity was diminished because its goal and vision had been so quickly abandoned.
3. Exceptional leaders. These leaders set clear and robust goals, invest the time to share the vision of the goal, and remain steadfast in their commitment to the goal even as circumstances change. These are the leaders who are very effective at strategic planning because their words and actions are aligned. They inspire others to commit to the shared vision and motivate others to put forth a great effort to achieve the mutually shared goal.

Exceptional leaders know there are two different types of goals they need to use for different purposes. Specifically, there are **SMART** goals and **BHAGs**. The **SMART** acronym stands for Specific, Measurable, Achievable, Realistic, and Time-bound. **BHAGs** are Big, Hairy, Audacious Goals.

SMART goals are popular for both leadership and personal development and are very effective. Goals that are specific and measurable have clarity about the end state and what steps need to be taken to get there. When goals are achievable anyone the goal will affect believes it can be obtained. It is no good to set a goal for a team if it cannot be achieved—the team will not put forth the effort necessary to be successful. Realistic goals are built upon common understandings and easily accepted. Realistic goals are grounded in what is known, not what might come in the future. Finally, time-bound goals are not open-ended. There must be some point in the future when the goal needs to be achieved; this creates a sense of urgency and common timeline.

BHAGs are not bound by the same constraints. These are the goals that will happen over the horizon. They are big, hairy, and audacious because they are working towards a future point that does not have a clear path to achievement. BHAGs are not linear processes, moving from one activity to the next to result in success. The point of the BHAG is to inspire others to be more than they think they could otherwise — to be more creative, resourceful, and productive. When Starbucks set a goal to be the world's leading brand, it was setting a BHAG. When Microsoft set a goal to have a computer on every desk and in every home, that was a BHAG. When John F. Kennedy set a goal to land a man on the moon and return him safely to Earth, that was a BHAG. When used correctly, a BHAG can be tremendously valuable because it is inspirational. When goal, vision, and strategy are aligned, they can produce exceptional results.

Take a moment to think about the two different types of goals that exceptional leaders use. Are you typically using SMART goals or BHAGs? Are you taking the time to think through all the necessary steps to ensure SMART goals are successful? Are your BHAGs sufficiently large and inspiring? To help develop your goal setting and visioning capacity as a leader, we recommend the following:

First, think of a BHAG that is appropriate to your role as a leader. You might not want to target landing a man on the moon, but your goal should be big enough to stretch beyond what you know you and your team can achieve today. Next, make sure your vision for the BHAG is crystal clear. Can you describe it to others and convey the same impact and meaning? It is not necessary to know how you will achieve the goal, but you must be clear on the desired end-state. When you have a clear vision of the end state, congratulations! You are taking the first steps necessary to be an exceptional leader, and demonstrating your ability to plan strategically.

After you have your BHAG vision, we recommend you create three SMART goals that support the vision. If the BHAG is the destination, the SMART goals are the map. This should not be a quick exercise. Developing three SMART goals should require significant thought and insight. What does your team need to accomplish to ultimately arrive at the BHAG destination? When you complete your SMART goals, make sure you can share a clear vision for each of them as well. What you are constructing is a plan for achieving a large and inspirational goal that is supported by specific, shorter-term, more concrete goals.

Exceptional leaders use this model because it works. There are other approaches that are successful. We strongly encourage you to experiment with different methods. However, as a practical guide, we want to make sure you have a proven model with a proven set of guidelines. As you work on developing your goal setting and visioning, try not to become too overwhelmed or discouraged with the process. It is difficult; this is why strategy consultants can charge such high rates! Try to keep the process simple without becoming stuck in the details. Focus on the goals and the vision for the end-state. As an exceptional leader, your ability to influence others will be related to your ability to inspire them and help them understand and commit to a shared vision. The more you work on developing this ability, the more natural it will become, and the more comfortable you will be with the strategic planning aspect of your leadership role.

PROBLEM SOLVING

As a leader, one of your most important roles will be to solve problems. It is surprising the number of leaders we have worked with over the years that get frustrated or agitated by the necessity to address and resolve problems. This always seems counterintuitive to us, because problem solving is core to being a leader. There is not a certain percentage of the role that you should expect to be associated with problem solving; instead, if you expect your entire role to be dedicated to problem solving, then any other time becomes a bonus.

We suggest this extreme perspective because the sooner you embrace its reality, the more successful and happy you will be as a leader. Think of it as moving from a cool, dry climate to a hot and humid one. When we moved from Colorado to Florida in the middle of the summer, we thought we might not ever get used to our new reality. We kept waiting for the heat and humidity to subside.

But relief didn't come when we wanted it. We had to embrace the fact that we were going to need to live with our new reality. When we realized this, stopped wishing for relief from the heat, and acknowledged that this was just the way the things were going to be, we became much happier and more comfortable in our new environment. If we had continued to be frustrated with the situation, we would only have made ourselves miserable. Fixating on what you cannot change is a recipe for misery. For a leader, solving problems is your reality.

For some, solving problems is a passion. Whether it is your own or others' problems doesn't matter. The satisfaction is in the process and results. For most of the leaders we have worked with, solving problems is a requirement but not a passion. For example, we work with the annual leadership program that helps prepare university personnel for administrative and leadership roles. Many participants want to move up and take on more leadership responsibility until they realize they no longer have the time to commit to other passion areas because all their time is tied up with solving problems. Instead of considering problem solving their most important responsibility, they consider it a waste of time and a distraction — and so they become miserable and ineffective.

For this reason, we suggest you embrace the mindset that problem solving is one of your primary responsibilities as a leader. Exceptional leaders acknowledge and appreciate this reality. They realize they must constantly demonstrate their problem-solving skills and engage others in collaborative and creative problem solving.

At this point, we encourage you to take a moment and reflect on your perspective on problem solving. If you are already in a leadership role, how do you view problem solving? Is it something you embrace or something you prefer to avoid? If you are not currently in a leadership role, are you ready to transition a significant amount of your effort away from your activities to solving problems, usually problems that are not directly your own? If you are struggling with embracing this perspective, think about what is necessary to influence a group of individuals to achieve a common goal. The goal is the destination; however, the journey along the way will include obstacles or challenges. These are the problems you, as a leader, are positioned to solve.

Mike Tyson famously said, "Everyone has a plan till they get punched in the mouth." Exceptional leaders understand that strategic planning is one of their most important responsibilities and that problem solving is the means to fulfill this responsibility. Problem solving addresses problems as they appear so when the punches start to fly, the plan is not abandoned.

To develop your problem-solving ability, we recommend you focus on three primary areas:

1. Shift your mindset from that of a technical expert to that of a well-connected generalist. When you become an exceptional leader, you must acknowledge that you will not be able to solve all problems yourself. Instead, you must be able to engage individuals who have the necessary knowledge and experience to solve what you cannot. This is the shift from specialist to generalist, technical competence to problem-solving competence. Exceptional leaders work very hard to know what they don't know. Blind spots can be damaging when trying to solve

problems, and one of the most effective ways to avoid this pitfall is to build a team of individuals who are smart, talented, and capable—and then rely on that team. When leaders tap the intelligence and resources of the right team members, they are demonstrating a high level of problem-solving capacity. We recommend you begin to build meaningful connections with the right technical experts so you will have access to the best possible insights.

2. Seek to understand the entire scope of the problem and then break it down into smaller parts. Take a two-step approach to problem solving. It is necessary to make sure you understand the big picture of the problem before breaking it down into smaller parts. When you take the time to fully understand the problem, the steps necessary to solve the problem become much more evident. This top-down approach helps ensure the right problem is being solved in the most efficient manner. As a leader, you should develop your own approach and level of comfort with how to accomplish this. You might be most comfortable breaking the problem into very ordered sub-problems that are all clearly identified and defined. Or you might prefer to break the problem down by generating lots of thoughts and ideas in a looser structure. Develop whatever approach that is comfortable for you, but make it one that allows you to understand the larger problem and to break it down into smaller parts.

3. Check in periodically to make sure that the problem you are solving is the root cause and not just a symptom. The less time you invest solving the wrong problem, the more effective you will be in solving the actual problem. This is a commonsense approach that exceptional leaders use to differentiate themselves from other leaders. For example, if the problem is that your team is not communicating well, a symptom might be

that there are not any emails between team members. The root problem is communication and the symptom is lack of emails. If you only addressed the email aspect, you might be very disappointed with the results. However, if you identified there was a lack of emails because there was a lack of communication which was rooted in a lack of trust among team members, a much more effective way to solve the problem would be to work on developing trust among the team.

As a leader, it is your responsibility to make sure you are addressing the root of the problem and not the symptom. The best way to make sure you are solving the root of the problem is to ask questions. Ask questions in a critical manner that challenges your understanding of the situation. Look for reasons why your assumptions might be inaccurate; hunt for other potential sources for the problem. The time spent confirming the root of the problem will be exponentially less than that spent chasing symptoms.

Exceptional leaders are exceptional problem solvers. They recognize that problem solving is one of the most important aspects of being a leader, and they look for opportunities to solve problems effectively. These leaders work on developing connections with a team of experts whom they can call upon when needed. Exceptional leaders also take the time to understand the problem at a high level, break it into smaller parts using a process that is comfortable for them, and periodically ensure they are addressing the root of the problem and not just symptoms. The more you work on developing these areas, the more comfortable you will be with solving problems as a leader—and, as a result, you will be more effective at strategic planning, because you will have the ability to overcome the unavoidable challenges and problems that arise along the way.

STAKEHOLDER ASSESSMENT

Imagine you want to drive from Denver to New York City. You do your research and know that you must drive east from your starting point to reach your eventual destination. You have calculated your estimated fuel economy and fuel budget. You have a good estimate of how long the drive will take. From a leadership perspective, these are the planning components necessary to give your journey the highest likelihood of success. You know where you want to go, what resources you need to get there, and approximately how long it will take.

This should be a familiar scenario, not only for anyone who has ever taken a road trip, but for anyone who has ever managed or led as well. In project management, these criteria are known as cost, quality, and time. Cost is the amount you budget for fuel. Quality is the miles per gallon. Finally, time is how long it takes to reach your destination.

Cost, quality, and time are the three considerations that drive project management. The goal is to focus on the two most important criteria, acknowledging that it is almost impossible to have all three. You might have a vehicle that is cheap and fast, but it will not be of the highest quality; or you might have a vehicle that is fast and of the highest quality, but is expensive. It is difficult, if not impossible, to have something fast, cheap, and of the highest quality.

Although this is an important note to make, this book is not focused on management; it is focused on leadership. As Peter Drucker said, "Management is doing things right; leadership is doing the right things." As a manager, it is appropriate to make sure you have considered the costs, time, and quality aspects of your journey; as a leader, you must make sure you are headed in the right direction.

If you get turned around and confused while leaving Denver and instead of driving east start driving west, does it matter what sort of fuel economy you have or how much time you have spent? Any fuel you burn will be wasted because it is taking you further from your intended destination. Exceptional leaders know that cost, time, and quality are necessary to track, but these criteria are insufficient measures for making it to the desired destination. These leaders know it is much better to find out they are going in the wrong direction after one mile than after 100 or 1,000 miles. Consequently, they assess the impact of their actions on the stakeholders.

The dictionary defines a stakeholder as, "One who is involved in or affected by a course of action." By the very nature of leading, interactions occur with other individuals. These other individuals are stakeholders in your leadership effort, because they are involved in or affected by your actions. For example, these individuals might provide the financial backing for your leadership if you are being paid to deliver a product or service by a third party. Or you might be representing the interests of these individuals if you are advocating for a policy change. Or stakeholders might be the members of your team working with you to achieve a common goal.

Stakeholder assessments are a very effective tool for strategic planning. Exceptional leaders know that assessing the impact of their actions can have a significant impact on their ability to plan and execute. Our research has shown that exceptional leaders approach stakeholder assessment using two primary approaches:

1. They periodically check in with stakeholders to see what impact their actions are having.
2. When the process is over, they take the time to reflect and assess the overall impacts of their actions. The insights gained from stakeholder assessments are then used to reinforce strategic plans and inform future planning efforts.

Within the academic discipline of evaluation, these assessment categories are known as *formative* and *summative*.

Leaders use formative assessments to make sure they are on the right track and that all stakeholders are bought in to the process and approach. If course corrections are necessary because of, for example, a misunderstanding on the desired destination, formative evaluation allows leaders to make the changes before going too far in the wrong direction. Over the years, we've been surprised that leaders think they understand the desired destination, plan, and then execute the plan without ever taking the time to check in along the way. Formative assessments are not a waste of time; they are critical to success. It would be like, in our driving example, never taking the time to consult a map or look at the road signs along the way. If you were only focused on your fuel economy, how much money you were spending, and how long the trip was lasting, you might find yourself in San Francisco rather than New York. This is an extreme example, but it happens in leadership all the time. As a leader, you must be committed to looking at the map and consulting the signs along the way to the destination.

Exceptional leaders give summative assessments once they reach their desired destinations. Summative assessments are used for reflection and learning. This is where an analysis of the plan versus the reality is conducted. Was the fuel economy consistent with expectations? Did the journey take longer or shorter than expected? Along the way, were course corrections necessary? What should be done differently in the future to improve the process or make it less painful?

It is also critical to make sure the process is reviewed and summarized with all the stakeholders involved. Are their outcomes consistent with their expectations? What did they think went well? What could be improved? Are there any suggestions for the type or frequency of formative assessments along the way?

To help develop your stakeholder assessment capacity, we suggest the following process:

1. When you start a leadership role, document anyone who might be involved with or affected by the course of action. Generally, this will include two categories: internal and external stakeholders.

    Internal stakeholders are those with whom you will have frequent and direct involvement, usually within the same organization. For example, everyone on your team is an internal stakeholder. If you are reporting to a supervisor within the same organization, they are an internal stakeholder. If your leadership role is not within a formal organization but leading a committee of volunteers, everyone on the committee should be considered an internal stakeholder.

    External stakeholders are anyone outside of your team or organization who may be affected, but who is not considered an internal stakeholder. External stakeholders may include a client, policy maker, or the group being represented. For example, if you are leading a committee of volunteers advocating for more funding for a youth program, external stakeholders include the policy makers you are advocating with, the youth program, and any other groups that are involved but not directly participating on the committee. Peer organizations that are also advocating for more youth program funding would be external stakeholders.

2. After you identify a comprehensive list of stakeholders, establish a stakeholder assessment plan. The plan should not be confused with the dreaded status meetings that fill up calendars. Status meetings tend to be a waste of time and just

a public recitation of management activities—cost, time, and quality. Exceptional leaders understand status meetings might be required for some situations, but they limit them as much as possible. Instead, the stakeholder assessment plan should be dynamic and have meaningful impact on all stakeholders involved.

We recommend a sequence in which external stakeholder assessments are used to inform internal stakeholder assessments. The view from the outside should serve as an impact check that is then used to make corrections as necessary. The internal assessment should reality-test views from the outside as well as offer insights and suggestions. We recommend the process be front loaded: conduct assessments more frequently at first with longer stretches of time between assessments as the journey matures. At the end of the process, the summative assessment should involve all stakeholders and ensure there is a common understanding of the outcomes as well as of the journey.

There is no formula for how stakeholder assessments should occur. The key point to remember is that exceptional leaders use stakeholder assessments to make sure they are working towards the right destination and to reflect and learn important lessons about the process when complete. Rather than try to provide specific guidelines, we recommend you develop your own process, one that works best for your situation. The more comfortable you become with the approach, the more likely you will use it in a manner that is effective for you. When used effectively, stakeholder assessments can be a powerful tool to support and inform strategic planning.

SUMMARY

Many leadership theories and books focus on the strategic planning aspects of leadership, and for good reason. Strategic planning is one of the areas that differentiate a leader from a manager, and an exceptional leader from everyone else. Exceptional leaders are not narrowly focused in their approach to strategic planning; instead, they understand it is a group of associated and complementary leadership dimensions. They also recognize that strategic planning is fundamentally connected to a common goal. It is difficult, if not impossible, to achieve a common goal without a strategic plan; and without a common goal, a strategic plan does not have any value. Exceptional leaders focus on the simplicity of the connection rather than on the burden of details.

In the context of leadership development, it is not necessary to dwell on concepts like game theory or other academic theories of strategy. There are fantastic books and resources that are available to assist if you are interested in learning more about strategy as a subject. The purpose of this chapter is to focus on the practical aspects of strategic planning that exceptional leaders use to set strategy, make plans, and overcome obstacles in pursuit of a common goal. When done effectively, strategic planning can look like precognition. The process is not magical, but it does take a dedicated effort.

In this chapter, we covered six capacities associated with strategic planning. We provided insights and recommendations on critical thinking, decision making, global and systems thinking, goal setting and visioning, problem solving, and stakeholder assessment. There might be areas where you feel as though you are already very skilled, and others where you don't feel like you have much experience. Where you are currently does not matter. Your current skill level (or exposure to strategic planning) is much less important than your willingness to put forth the effort and work on developing your ability to strategically plan. The key is to begin the journey. As you gain experience and confidence, you will find that you are naturally able to strategically plan more effectively. When you develop the necessary capacity, you will find that you can comfortably use more sophisticated approaches. However, you must take the responsibility to begin.

SUPPORTING

Anyone can hold the helm when the sea is calm
— *Publilius Syrus*

One of the ways leadership differs from other forms of power is that leadership is earned. You can only lead others if they are willing to be led. Anyone can accumulate power with enough resources. You can force others to obey through coercion or other abusive measures; however, being powerful does not make you a leader.

Managers have power based on their position and the ability to impose punishments and rewards. Leaders have power because others are willing to be influenced by them. This is not to imply that managers can't also be leaders; however, a powerful position does not automatically equate to leadership. Leaders don't rely on positions to lead. Leaders can be higher, lower, or at a peer level within a hierarchy. Some of the most famous leaders in history had nothing to do with positions. Joan of Arc was an 18-year-old peasant girl who led the French to a military victory over the English.

Leaders are those people who are willing to commit themselves and put in the time and effort to accomplish a common goal. Exceptional leaders are those who are willing to give the credit for accomplishments and take the blame for failures. This is the path necessary to becoming an exceptional leader and is part of the reason so many people are satisfied with being adequate leaders or leaders in name only.

Exceptional leaders provide ongoing support to others. John F. Kennedy once described a farmer as someone, "Who has to buy everything he buys at retail—sell everything he sells at wholesale—and pay the freight both ways." This description is consistent with support required from exceptional leaders. As an exceptional leader, any problems become your problems, and it is your responsibility to be aware of the world around you while responding to the needs of those you are leading.

Leading is a big responsibility. There are too many quick-fix leadership concepts out there that completely neglect the importance and gravity of this responsibility. From our experience and research, we have found anything worth doing will require effort on your part. The good news is there is no limitation to who can become an exceptional leader. We guarantee you can become an exceptional leader if you are willing to put forth the effort.

Throughout this chapter, we will cover the five dimensions of supporting: conflict management, fostering and enabling others, issue awareness, political process awareness, and recognizing values.

Leading can be a very rewarding experience; however, to lead effectively, you must be willing to work hard. Exceptional leaders work hard and support others to achieve a common goal.

CONFLICT MANAGEMENT

Without taking too long to think about it, what comes to mind when you hear the word *conflict*? Chances are you thought about anger—people arguing and screaming at each other. Or perhaps you thought about military battles or wars. Do you tend to think of conflict as positive or negative? Is conflict something that you would prefer to engage in or something you would prefer to avoid? There is no right or wrong answer to these questions; they are just your perceptions. The point is not to pass any sort of judgment, but rather to acknowledge where you are currently.

Most perceive conflict as a negative activity that should be avoided. As a culture, the term "conflict" tends to be regarded as something undesirable and destructive. This is not necessarily inaccurate, depending on how conflict is defined. The dictionary defines conflict as "A fight, battle, or struggle, especially a prolonged struggle; strife." In the spirit of maintaining good relations and minimizing tensions, it is logical that most individuals would prefer to avoid this definition of conflict. Conflict defined in this manner is meant to tear down and break things apart; it is destructive in nature.

An alternate definition of conflict is, "Discord of action, feeling, or effect; antagonism or opposition, as of interests or principles." This is a completely different perspective on conflict. Think about how a blade is made. There is a raw material, like iron or steel, that is formed into a rough shape. The rough shape is then worked and honed, improving the sharpness during each stage of the process. Think about each stage and successive improvement as a form of conflict. There is energy expended, there is a change experienced; however, the change is constructive in nature. Eventually, the conflict transforms the raw material into something that is perfected. It would be impossible to take a lump of iron and turn it into a blade without constructive effort.

Here are two definitions for the same word that have very different interpretations, one destructive and one constructive. As a leader, it is critical that you acknowledge these two different forms of conflict. Exceptional leaders are those who demonstrate a respect for conflict and use it to learn, grow, and change. To do so, these leaders take three primary perspectives when managing conflict.

Exceptional leaders:

- Determine whether the conflict is constructive or destructive.
- Use different approaches to managing the conflict depending on the situation.
- Cultivate a culture that expects and respects constructive conflict.

Managing conflict is one of the most powerful ways a leader can support others. There are few activities less productive than destructive conflict and few activities more valuable than constructive conflict. Exceptional leaders understand this reality and do not shy away from either form of conflict, although they are also careful to appropriately categorize the conflict. From a practical perspective, we would recommend the following guideline:

Any conflict that is personal-based is destructive, and any conflict that is idea-based is constructive.

This may seem like a very basic guideline, and it is. The point is not to develop a 50-point checklist for classifying conflict situations. The point is to give you a starting point so that you can lead more effectively, and practice and develop your own set of standards and criteria for classifying conflict. We have found that one of the reasons leaders are conflict-averse is they consider all conflict as a negative and so take an ostrich approach: stick their head in the sand and pretend the conflict doesn't exist. Exceptional leaders behave differently. These leaders don't shy away from conflict; they embrace it and take the necessary steps to address it.

Exceptional leaders use different approaches to manage conflict depending on the situation and type of conflict (constructive or destructive). Again, we are going to suggest a set of basic guidelines. Exceptional leaders do not need to be certified mediators or negotiators, but they do need to have a general set of operating principles so they are comfortable with different conflict situations.

When exceptional leaders recognize a destructive conflict situation, they rapidly intervene to shut the conflict down. For example, we were once working with a very dysfunctional volunteer board. There were two board members who disliked each other, and every time the board got together, these two found something to argue about. These arguments usually started over a piece of business the board was discussing but quickly deteriorated into personal attacks. The board chairperson was conflict averse, and so every time a conflict arose, she quietly sat back and let the two tear into each other.

What was surprising to us, in addition to the sight of two highly respected members of the community going at each other, was the way the rest of the committee reacted. It was clear that this behavior had become so common that the rest of the board simply stopped what they were doing and ignored the two until they eventually stopped. Sometimes this would be a minute or two, sometimes five or more. The destructive conflict had been tolerated for so long that it had metastasized. The board was broken and suffering as a consequence.

To address the issue, we coached the board chair to immediately stop the meeting the next time the two diverged from the topic under discussion. It was the chair's responsibility to point out to these individuals that their conflict was having a negative effect on the group, and that the only form of conflict that would be tolerated was that related to issues. This was a big undertaking for the typically conflict-averse chair; however, the future of the board was at stake, and if she couldn't manage the conflict, the board was likely to disband. At the next meeting, when the two individuals started to diverge from the topic, the chair shocked them both by speaking up, asserting herself and letting them know that this form of conflict would no longer be tolerated. Although they were respected members of the community, they would be asked to leave the board if they did not quit. Shocked silence from the two members and the entire board ensued. The frankness of the approach did not provide any space for misinterpretation. By clearly and immediately addressing the destructive conflict, the chair managed the situation and began the process of rebuilding the board.

Leaders sometimes struggle with this frankness, because it seems too simple. Surely there must be some sort of multi-step process required when it comes to dealing with destructive conflict? Nope. Clarity and simplicity eliminate complexity and ambiguity. Exceptional leaders do not tolerate destructive conflict. They take clear and decisive steps to make sure everyone knows and understands this perspective. One of the ways exceptional leaders address destructive conflict is to redirect the situation back to constructive conflict—conflict that is focused on ideas, not people.

When an exceptional leader either recognizes constructive conflict or is successful in redirected destructive conflict, they view it as a tremendous opportunity. Unlike destructive conflict, which needs to be stopped immediately, constructive conflict should be nurtured and cultivated. There are many different conflict management styles, which are a result of natural inclinations and past experiences with conflict. The truth is there is no single best approach to conflict management. Every conflict situation is happening in a context. Therefore, not every conflict management approach can be win-win.

Regardless of their conflict management approach, exceptional leaders use constructive conflict situations as an opportunity to learn, grow, and change. They do so by being adaptable, collaborative, and inquisitive. Generally, exceptional leaders start with a win-win mindset so both sides of the conflict can gain from the situation. However, exceptional leaders are not paralyzed by the need to artificially create win-win situations. Have you ever heard the saying, "A camel is a horse designed by committee"? When everyone gets some of what they want, the net result can be less elegant than a more decisive approach. Exceptional leaders understand that a win-win approach is ideal, but not if it is detrimental to achieving the common goal. If you remain focused on ideas and start with a win-win mindset, your constructive conflict management approach will naturally emerge.

Finally, exceptional leaders cultivate a culture that expects, and respects, constructive conflict. Elie Wiesel said, "The opposite of love is not hate, it's indifference. The opposite of art is not ugliness, it's indifference. The opposite of faith is not heresy, it's indifference. And the opposite of life is not death, it's indifference." A culture without constructive conflict is cultivating indifference. Constructive conflict stirs emotions, forces positions, and creates passion. When centered around ideas, conflict situations are powerful and highly desirable experiences. Sometimes, exceptional leaders will take a contrarian position to incite constructive conflict. Sometimes, they will juxtapose ideas to force a reaction. The point is not to agitate the situation but to sharpen the blade. To hone a piece of raw iron into something that is perfect. This process requires action. Action in the form of constructive conflict can have the same effect on ideas: honing them and perfecting them.

We recommend you spend some time contemplating your perspectives on conflict management. Focus on the distinction between constructive and destructive conflict and how as a leader you want to support others by managing both appropriately. Try to keep the concepts simple to begin with. Develop a practical mentality and give yourself permission to be uncomfortable. Along the way, you will inevitably make mistakes. The key is to keep practicing. Over time, you will develop a conflict management approach that works well for you. The sooner you can develop conflict resolution leadership capacity, the sooner you can support others more effectively.

FOSTERING AND ENABLING OTHERS

Personal development is a fantastic goal. We are strong believers in the importance of building skills or capacities that are for your own benefit. Whether for intellectual, health, or spiritual reasons, personal development can make you feel better, be happier, and live a more enjoyable life. However, as the name implies, personal development is focused on developing yourself. It is a self-oriented process, as it should be. On the contrary, leadership development should not be self-oriented. You should not lead for your own benefit, but for those you are leading. Many leadership theories and approaches do not acknowledge this distinction; consequently, what others have classified as leadership development is personal development.

Exceptional leaders recognize that improving themselves is a nice by-product of their larger aim, which is to lead and serve others more effectively. These leaders understand that, unlike personal development, leadership development is about doing what is necessary to lead others, not about doing what makes them feel comfortable or satisfied.

Think about the following scenario: a group of five individuals is on a camping trip in the woods, and night is approaching. They need to collect firewood and make a fire so they will have light and warmth after the sun goes down. If one individual volunteers to get firewood and only returns with enough wood for a small personal fire for themselves, is that leadership? Of course not. This would be selfish behavior that didn't benefit the group. On the other hand, if the volunteer came back with enough firewood to build a huge fire for everyone to enjoy, is that leadership? Leaders take the steps necessary to benefit the group, not just themselves.

From the perspective of benefiting the group, it is logical that exceptional leaders see the value and importance of fostering and enabling others. Developing skills and capacities to lead others more effectively is valuable; teaching others the skills and capacities so they too can be more effective leaders has exponentially more value. Chances are you have heard the quote from Maimonides, "Give a man a fish and you feed him for a day; teach a man to fish and you feed him for a lifetime." The same premise applies to leadership development. Becoming a better leader is great, but fostering and enabling others to become better leaders is even more powerful. Additionally, fostering and enabling others is directly related to a leader's ability to support others.

There are two primary steps exceptional leaders take to foster and enable others:

1. Fostering and enabling others to demonstrate the skills necessary to act as a leader by working with diverse groups, organizations, and communities to develop solutions and address a common goal. This is where the dynamics of leadership are so important to acknowledge. The first step is directed at supporting, but is a consequence of action, serving as a leader, and relationships and character—providing a model of leadership behavior and connecting with others. It would be illogical to try to support and enable others if you didn't first demonstrate the desired capacities and then take the time to get to know the people to whom you were modeling. Very few of us enjoy being told what to do, especially if we are told to do something for our own good. Exceptional leaders understand this dynamic and take the preliminary steps necessary to make sure any attempts at fostering and enabling are well-received and appreciated.

    To demonstrate and model effective leadership, we recommend working with a diversity of others, not just those with whom you share a common background or education. This will improve your credibility and help you acknowledge and appreciate what makes each individual unique and special. As a result, you will be able to connect with others more effectively and provide them the right sort of enablement opportunities. We recommend you work on making sure that, as a leader, you are getting to know everyone with whom you work as an individual. You need to learn what motivates them and what sort of leadership development they are interested in. The better you understand the needs of others, the more effectively you can support them.

2. Within situations, delegating responsibilities when appropriate, and enabling and strengthening others by sharing power and discretion. We have found that the first step is usually very easy for leaders to understand and implement. The second step is where most leaders, especially new leaders, struggle. One of the groups we work with is for new administrators in colleges and universities. Usually, these are successful faculty members who have been promoted into leadership positions. As faculty members, they were successful publishing journal articles, securing grant funding, and teaching classes. However, after taking on their new administrative position, they struggle. In the past, they might have been able to do everything necessary for their job themselves. They didn't have to rely on others to meet deadlines or milestones, so they became very good at taking care of everything.

As leaders, they struggle because their new roles make it impossible for them to use the independent approaches they relied on in the past. Now, they ought to work with others to accomplish everything. However, we have worked with individuals who are willing to put in over 80 hours a week to try to do it all by themselves rather than embrace the power and importance of delegation!

Exceptional leaders know that delegating responsibilities to others is not only necessary for managing their own workloads but critical for providing developmental opportunities. When these leaders share power and discretion, they are enabling others to act. As a leader, it is your responsibility to make sure you are providing the right sort of model and to understand the wants and needs of others. If you have done this correctly and provided appropriate and thoughtful delegation opportunities, it is time to trust those you have enabled.

This is a simplistic view of delegation, because the reality is that it is hard to turn things over to someone else. Instead of viewing delegation as purely a means to accomplish a goal, exceptional leaders also view it as a necessary process to foster and enable others. If the results of delegated projects are not viewed as either correct or incorrect, but rather as growth and learning opportunities, delegation is much less stressful.

To build your fostering and enabling of others' capacities, we recommend you start by thinking about how and what you are currently delegating. If you are not in a leadership position that offers opportunities to delegate to others, think about non-leadership situations. For example, are you the only person in your house who can do the laundry correctly? Or make lunch the way you like it? Any activity that you feel only you can do is a potential candidate for delegation. After thinking about what you are currently delegating and what you could potentially delegate, try to think about what is holding you back. Do you want to retain control? Are the stakes too high if something goes wrong? Had you never thought about delegating to someone else? Whatever the reason, try to determine whether you might feel comfortable trying to delegate more.

We recommend you start with something small. It is counter-productive to move too far too fast. If others don't have the skills and abilities to accomplish an activity, delegating it will be a failure and could cause more harm than good. Instead, start small and see what is beneficial and uncomfortable about the process. Remember, this is not just for your personal development, but also for others. The more you practice delegating, the more you will develop a gauge for benefits compared to drawbacks. We are not suggesting exceptional leaders delegate everything. However, exceptional leaders know that one of their main responsibilities is supporting others, and one of the best ways they can accomplish this is by fostering and enabling them through delegation.

ISSUE AWARENESS

Leadership is not a theoretical exercise; it happens in the real world, where experience and outcomes are often very dependent on the environment. The Roman philosopher Seneca famously said, "Luck is what happens when preparation meets opportunity." Exceptional leaders are those who are comfortable creating an environment in which opportunity and challenges occur. They work hard to ensure they are prepared to take advantage of opportunities as well as address challenges without losing sight of the common goal. From the outside, the success that exceptional leaders enjoy can look like luck.

If you knew the price of electricity was going to double in the next six months, what would you do? First, you'd probably look at how much you were paying currently as well as how you were using electricity. You might consider replacing old or inefficient appliances and changing old incandescent lights into fluorescent or LED bulbs. You would probably look at your monthly budget and figure out how you were going to pay the bill once the price increase occurred. You might also use the situation as a chance to examine your other monthly bills. Maybe you could find a way to reduce your monthly phone bill. All this preparation would seem like unnecessary effort to anyone who didn't know the price increase was coming; however, once the price doubled, your efforts would look brilliant. Instead of being caught unaware by the issue, you took steps to reduce your risk and maximize your opportunity. Maybe because of your success in reducing your monthly bills, you decide to offer your services as a consultant to your friends and colleagues. Now instead of just trying to figure out how to manage the issue, you have created a new opportunity.

What separates exceptional leaders from other leaders is they recognize that part of their responsibility in supporting others is to be aware of the issues that might affect their ability to reach a common goal. We consider issue awareness a supporting activity because, when done properly, it shifts the burden of the task from everyone else to the leader. When a leader takes on this responsibility, it gives cognitive capacity back to everyone else so they may focus on what is most important for them.

Think about the last time you flew on an airplane. For most of us, our last flight was probably with a commercial carrier and went like this: we bought our ticket, went to the airport, checked our luggage, stood in the security line, waited at the gate, and eventually boarded the plane. Although the process can be stressful, our responsibilities are limited. For us to get on the plane and fly from point A to point B, all we need to do was get on the plane; we don't have to review weather maps or register flight plans. We don't have to perform a walk around and look for mechanical issues. Once in the air, we don't have to worry about cruising altitude, turbulence, or any other updates or instructions that are being communicated to the pilots from the ground. The pilots are supporting our ability as passengers to move from point A to point B by taking care of these activities and by being aware of any issues that arise. As passengers, we can focus on other things, like reading, sleeping, and working on our laptops.

One of the amazing benefits of issue awareness is that when done properly, it not only allows leaders to support others, it also informs leaders' ability to plan. Issue awareness is one of the leadership dimensions that have benefits across many different areas.

How exceptional leaders go about staying aware of issues is as varied as the different goals that leaders are working towards. There is no single method or approach that works best, but there are some general guidelines. Specifically, exceptional leaders stay aware of local, national, and global issues through reading, research, questioning, and writing.

Based on this guideline, we have two main recommendations to help you develop your own issue awareness approach:

1. Focus on a breadth of issues to begin, followed by going deeper in specific areas.
2. Use your issue awareness actively, as it should not be passive knowledge.

When we work with leaders, and they come to understand how important issue awareness is to their ability to support others, one of the first questions we get is, "Where do I begin?" With technology and 24-hour-a-day news cycles, it is impossible for anyone to be fully informed all the time, let alone a leader who is trying to balance countless other responsibilities. From a practical perspective, we recommend the following approach to improving your issue awareness:

Commit to taking 15 minutes a day, ideally in the morning, to review a reputable newspaper. This can be either print or online; however, we recommend a print version. This suggestion came from a former congressional researcher who spent decades working with Congress in Washington, D.C. The reason print newspapers from reputable sources are preferable is they make the news cycle finite. Instead of scrolling through headlines online or on your phone, you can quickly scan all the headlines in a newspaper, including local, business, international, and other sections in 15 minutes. If there are interesting articles, you should read them, though this will add time. Since the newspaper is a physical object, when you are done with the paper, you are done. There is not yet one more link at the bottom of the screen to consume more of your time.

The other reason we recommend reputable newspapers is they still hold to journalistic standards that include fact checking and source verification. We recognize that print newspapers may not be an option for you based on your location or personal preferences, so you may need to find an online version. This is completely fine; just try to remember that it is important to get a good overview of the headlines daily and not get distracted by suggested links and the inevitable time vortex that follows.

In addition to daily headlines, we recommend you find at least one magazine or industry journal to read monthly. If you don't know where to begin, just do a Google search; you will find both trade and academic resources that you didn't know existed. Try to take at least two hours a month and focus on becoming aware of the issues that are most relevant to you. Whether the information is printed or available online does not matter; however, be sure it is from a reputable source. Like newspapers, these periodicals have longer publishing cycles, so there is usually more time for fact-checking and confirmation. Gaining deeper insights on goal specific issues can be very helpful to your ability to support others.

These two recommendations are very simple for a reason: if you try to do too much too quickly, it is very likely you will become overwhelmed and frustrated and give up. To begin with, the goal is to go a mile wide and an inch deep. As you read the headlines every day and dive into the occasional article, you will see trends emerge. Maybe the cost of commodities is rising or falling, or there is a new policy under consideration that may affect your industry. When you combine this daily high-level overview with the industry-specific insights of a monthly periodical, the result can be very powerful—which leads us to the second recommendation.

In addition to the ongoing efforts to stay aware of issues, exceptional leaders read, research, question, and write. A secret that educators know is that one of the best ways to learn a topic is to teach it. This is the same principle that exceptional leaders use when it comes to issue awareness. These individuals don't just accumulate knowledge passively; they look for ways to use it.

The practical aspect of the first step is to develop a base of issue awareness, which will take some time. Once you have an established base of issue awareness, look for opportunities to apply it. For example, say you are a leader in an import export industry and have just learned about a proposed policy that will increase the taxes on imported goods by 50%. This could have huge impact on your industry, so it is an issue that is very important to you. However, awareness is not sufficient; you must take the steps necessary to use this awareness. Consequently, you might read and research more about the proposed policy. Which countries are involved? What problem is the tax intended to solve? Who is proposing the policy? What is their interest in the policy? You continue to ask questions and probe deeper. In addition, you might begin writing or using the awareness you are gathering. Maybe use your communication skills to post to social media or explain the situation to others. The key is to use your issue awareness in a way that is supportive to others and helps accomplish your common goal.

The more aware you become of the issues that you might face, the more you can do to prepare and hopefully capitalize on these opportunities.

On your journey to becoming an exceptional leader, there are many different areas that you will need to develop; issue awareness is a foundational capacity that will be very helpful in your ability to support others effectively. It is not necessary that you become an issues expert overnight; however, you must be willing to begin the process and start to become aware of issues starting today. The more you practice, the more comfortable you will be with developing an approach that works best for you.

POLITICAL PROCESS AWARENESS

Before beginning the next section, we would like you to take a moment and think about the word "politics." What comes to mind? Maybe "politics" brings about negative images—images of smoke-filled back rooms where power brokers glad-hand and make deals. Or perhaps you have a very different perspective—perhaps you think of transparency and civic engagement. Both viewpoints, and any in between, are completely valid. There is not a right or wrong answer. Like most leadership activities, the key is to recognize that nothing is clear cut. However, it is important to acknowledge your preconceived notions before proceeding, because your initial perception can have a very large impact on your openness to learning and developing.

Another common response when we ask about politics is to focus on office politics. At its core, office politics revolve around power and influence, and so is closely related to the leadership process. Although office politics is a relevant topic for leaders, it is not the focus for this section. Instead, this section focuses on legislative politics. Office politics are organically addressed throughout the book—that is, the suggestions and capacities we provide will have an immediate impact on your ability to identify and navigate office politics. Office politics can change almost overnight; leadership endures. As an exceptional leader, your skills and capabilities are not limited to your ability to play the office politics game, and will provide real and meaningful value consistently over time.

Regardless of political opinions, exceptional leaders recognize that they must be aware of the political process, and of legislative politics in particular. For many leaders, especially those who are early in their leadership journey, the connection to politics seems far removed. The legislation that is occurring at the local, state, or national level seems to have little impact on their ability to perform as a leader.

Exceptional leaders recognize how shortsighted and limiting this perspective can be. The political process can have a tremendous impact on a leader's ability to plan, take action, and anticipate change. It is like having access to a seven-day weather forecast and not taking the time to see what the coming days might look like before planning a picnic. However, unlike a weather forecast, which you have no ability to influence, the political process gives you a chance to impact the outcome.

There are two primary areas where exceptional leaders differentiate themselves from other leaders when it comes to their political process awareness. Exceptional leaders:

1. Make sure they understand the political process at the local, state, and national level.
2. Assess the political scene and political decision-making process and think about how it can influence them or those they work with and around.

Imagine you own a home in a residential neighborhood in a quiet part of town. One day, you notice that the empty lot behind your home where your kids like to play baseball has a 'Land Use Planning Notice' sign. You recognize the county sign as a necessary public notice for a proposed zoning change in your county. Because this is something that directly affects where you live, you note the phone number on the sign and call the zoning board. When you talk to the zoning board, you find out that an application has been filed to rezone the lot from residential to commercial. Instead of a quiet empty lot, the space could be turned into a warehouse with large trucks coming and going around the clock.

How do you respond to this situation? There are many possible next steps; the key is to improve your understanding and act. For example, an exceptional leader might find out when the public hearing is scheduled before the county commissioners and what sort of comments the zoning board is soliciting from those potentially impacted by the proposed change. They could then organize a group of neighbors willing to speak at the meeting and voice their concerns over the proposed change. They might also meet with the county commissioners personally and explain how the change could increase noise and danger while lowering property values. They could start a petition to capture the names of other concerned citizens whom the change might affect. These actions would have infinitely more impact than taking no action at all—and the only way to know which actions to take is to understand the process.

Based on the provided example, think about how the political process might affect other areas where you lead. Now ask yourself if there are areas where your business might be impacted. What if, instead of rezoning the political process was considering increased taxes on businesses like yours? Or mandating additional certifications or licensing? There are many ways the political process might affect your ability to lead.

Getting involved in politics may seem like a large undertaking, one that requires the right connections and years of experience. But although the right connections and years of experience don't hurt, they are not necessary. We recommend you work to understand the political process at all levels by following the same basic steps:

1. Find out how you are represented in the process. Who are your county commissioner, state representative, and national

representative?
2. Find a local issue or policy that interests or impacts you. Find out everything you can on the issue. If it is specific policy, find out who is sponsoring the policy and why. What are some of the potential consequences of the policy?
3. Think about how the policy might impact your ability to lead. Will the new policy be good for you and your situation or make it more difficult?
4. Schedule a meeting with the appropriate political representative to discuss the impact of the policy on you.

That's it. Not that complicated, right?

If you take the time to understand the basics, and then have the courage to begin, you can rapidly improve your understanding. We recommend you start now, when you don't necessarily have an urgent situation that you need to deal with, so in the future you will be well prepared when the stakes are higher.

The second area where exceptional leaders distinguish themselves is in their ability to assess the political scene and political decision-making process at all levels. This is the point at which these leaders combine their understanding of the political process with their insights and experience. Exceptional leaders assess the political scene and the political decision-making process by consistently showing up and being engaged. They stay informed of issues and policies; they watch for trends and they think about potential impacts. We recommend you work on your ability to assess the political scene and the political decision-making process by becoming more engaged and informed on the issues and policies facing your ability to lead. This includes looking at what new policies might come about, as well as previous policies that are now affecting you.

In his book *Outliers: The Story of Success*, Malcom Gladwell states,

"The 10,000-hour rule is a definite key in success." We don't expect you will spend 10,000 hours to become one of the foremost experts on assessing the political scene; however, we guarantee if you spend 10 to 100 hours engaged in the political process, and actively working to develop your ability to assess the political scene, you will experience a significant improvement. Over time, you will be able to nurture this ability to become even more comfortable and confident, further positioning yourself to be a tremendous resource and an exceptional leader.

RECOGNIZING VALUES

Chances are you have heard the term "values" in the context of leadership. This is such an overused word that it has almost lost its meaning. Take a moment to think about the word *values*. How would you define it? After you have a rough definition in mind, think about the following questions: Was it hard or easy to come up with a definition? Is your definition simple or complex? Does your definition work under multiple conditions? For example, does your definition apply to leadership situations as well as personal situations? Finally, do you think if you gave your definition to someone else, they would be able to understand and agree?

Everyone's definition of this word is unique, and has unique emphasis, although the various definitions usually have similarities. For example, many include "it depends." Since everyone's definition is slightly different, let's go with a basic dictionary definition: "Relative worth, utility, or importance." At its most basic level, leadership values equate to the worth we put into something. Generally, these are concepts, not physical objects. For example, if you value your integrity above everything else, then there is nothing you would be willing to accept if it meant you had to compromise your integrity — no amount of money, fame, or prestige. If you value your family above all else, there is nothing that you would be willing to accept if it meant you had to compromise your family — or whatever family means to you. The point is not to get stuck in the details; the point is to acknowledge that values are based on worth and that as a leader, it is necessary to not only know your own values, but also to recognize the values of others.

Exceptional leaders demonstrate clear personal values and set examples for others by aligning their actions with the common values of the organization and those they are leading. In so doing, exceptional leaders demonstrate stewardship of those they are leading. When a leader's values are clear and well understood, aligned with the values of others, and consistent with their actions, they can provide an exceptional level of support.

To assist you in developing the capacity to recognize values, we suggest three primary steps:

1. Take the time to clarify your personal and leadership values.
2. Check to ensure your actions are consistent with your values.
3. Assess others' values and make sure there is alignment.

Let's look at these in a little more detail.

The first step to developing your capacity to recognize values is to determine your own personal values. You probably already have a good sense for what these are, but taking the time to clarify and be explicit will be helpful. Don't worry if this task feels a bit overwhelming; values are so meaningful to us that it is supposed to feel difficult to define them — this is just a consequence of the richness, complexity, and beauty of being human. To help you along, we suggest you start with the nine core values Lynn Kahle identified in his book, *Social Values and Social Change: Adaptation to Life in America*: self-respect, security, warm relationships with others, self-fulfillment, a sense of accomplishment, being respected, a sense of belonging, fun and enjoyment, and excitement. Use these as a starting point, but don't feel limited by this list. You might find that you value, for example, health, the environment, human rights, freedom, or financial success—or not. Your values should be your own.

We recommend you start by writing down a list of your top 20 values. Stretch beyond what you might think of easily. Once you have your list, take some time to think about each value—and specifically, what would it take for you to compromise on the value? The point in this process is to be honest, not judgmental. For example, if you have a value on health, but can never find the time to take care of yourself, the worth you place on the value is less than the worth you place on other values; consequently, you are willing to compromise on this value. This is not a bad thing; this is just honest. Next, go through your list and try to cut the list in half. You should do this based on the worth you place on each value. If you started with a list of 20, your goal is to work down to a list of 10.

Take a moment and look at your shortened list. Try not to think about what you eliminated, only on what remains. Again, go through and think about the worth you place on each value. Again, try to cut the list in half, moving from 10 down to 5 values in your list. This should be a challenging process, so give yourself the time and space necessary to work it through.

Finally, take your list of 5 values, and focus on only those 5 values. With that list of 5, try to cut the list down to 2 or 3 top values. These should be the values that are worth so much to you that you are unwilling to compromise on them. This should be a very intensive process, one that might take a long time and considerable self-reflection. However, when you reach this point, congratulations! You will have achieved a level of self-awareness and insight very few ever achieve. Exceptional leaders are those who are willing to invest the time to recognize these.

Take a moment to think about only the values you are unwilling to compromise. Are your actions aligned to these values? Are the values consistent with the values of those you are trying to serve? If the answer to both questions is yes, you are recognizing values and performing as an exceptional leader in this area. However, if you were not able to answer yes to both questions, or if you were not able to answer the second question at all, you will need to spend time thinking about how to address these gaps.

If your actions are not aligned with your values, you have the opportunity right now to decide to change. We are not implying this change will be easy or happen overnight; however, all that is required is for you to make a choice. When you can make difficult choices, you are embracing the responsibilities that come along with being an exceptional leader.

If your values are not aligned with the values of those you lead, you need to honestly assess whether the misalignment is major or minor. If it is a major misalignment, you need to consider whether this leadership role is the right one for you. Being a leader gives you the opportunity to influence others' values, but there are certain limitations to how and why you would want to do so. There is not a scale to decide what difference is too much, or whether value misalignments should be addressed. As an exceptional leader, you must have the personal insight and authentic self-awareness to be able to make these decisions.

If you are not sure how your values align with others', we recommend you invest the time in trying to uncover this information. If your main value is personal fulfillment, and you don't know that everyone else's main value is financial success, you may struggle with leading effectively. Here, too, is a situation where the solution is usually simple. Rather than try to guess or make assumptions, we recommend you ask. Asking might include personal conversations or surveys or some other way to gather the information in an appropriate way. As a leader, you should know the best way to go about getting at this information, given your leadership context. The important part is to begin the process and ask.

When you know what your values are, act in alignment with those values, and lead according to the common values shared with the organization or others you are leading, you are demonstrating stewardship. According to the dictionary, stewardship is, "The careful and responsible management of something entrusted to one's care." We can't think of a more appropriate definition for what exceptional leaders do, especially when it comes to recognizing values and supporting others.

SUMMARY

Exceptional leaders are those who know it is their responsibility not only to lead, but also to support others. There are certain responsibilities that a leader must take on, because they improve the condition for everyone. Whether it is developing their issue and political process awareness to be adequately prepared for the benefit of others, or managing conflict in a productive manner, supporting others covers a very broad set of obligations. These are not all glory-filled activities; many of them happen behind the scenes and are never seen by others. However, this hard work is what differentiates exceptional leaders from everyone else. They earn their recognition as a leader by taking blame and giving credit, and by being willing to work hard to support others, no matter the outcome.

For some, supporting others may come as second nature. You naturally give and derive happiness by seeing others succeed and be happy. For others, giving and supporting others without expected return may feel uncomfortable. Both natural dispositions are normal. Regardless of your predisposition, you can be very effective in supporting others as a leader. You must first honestly assess where you are currently and where you need to improve. Once you identify these areas, you need to put forth the effort to practice and develop these capacities. Through an ongoing process of learning, practice, and reflection, you will find that you are more and more comfortable and effective at supporting others.

We included five capacities for supporting others in this chapter. We covered conflict management, fostering and enabling others, issue awareness, political process awareness, and recognizing values. Supporting others as a leader is a broad topic that might have easily included capacity areas that ultimately ended up in different chapters throughout this book. However, even though supporting others is less focused than some of the other areas, it is no less important. If anything, the breadth of the topic should indicate the need for you to ensure you are spending an adequate amount of time developing yourself as a leader in this area. The hard work you dedicate to supporting others will help tremendously on your journey to becoming an exceptional leader.

In the next chapter, we cover the coordinating aspect of exceptional leaders. Leadership requires the interaction with others; therefore, the most effective leaders are those who can coordinate others effectively. Exceptional leaders know that, unlike management, which focuses on directing, effective coordinating requires more nuanced and specialized capacities.

COORDINATING

Of all the things I've done, the most vital is coordinating those who work with me and aiming their efforts at a certain goal.
—*Walt Disney*

If strategic planning is the show horse of leadership, coordinating is the work horse.

All roles have activities that are essential but not particularly glamorous. They're the activities that keep the machinery running and the lights on. They're the overlooked necessities that no one thinks about until something goes wrong.

Coordinating is like the oil that keeps an engine running smoothly. It keeps all the parts working together in harmony, quietly circulating through the system. The oil may not be the reason the cylinders fire in sequence or the rotor turns; however, the oil is the reason why all these parts can perform their assigned roles effectively. Without oil in an engine, parts can easily overheat and grind together, causing the engine to break down. When this happens, it is usually too late. The damage to the engine can be costly or impossible to repair. For this reason, refreshing and maintaining the oil level is critical.

Just like oil in an engine, the coordinating aspect of leadership is responsible for addressing many of the intangibles that are necessary for others to perform their roles effectively—making sure that everything is cared for so others can accomplish what they need to. Like maintaining the oil in an engine, exceptional leaders know they have a responsibility to maintain those they lead by effectively coordinating efforts and activities.

Coordinating is very similar to the management concept of directing. Directing is based on authority and the power associated with a superior position. To be clear, we are not intending to be derogatory about project management. These are critical responsibilities that help to make sure projects are completed on time and on budget. However, sometimes leaders struggle to see the difference between project management and coordinating. To clarify, we would propose the following examples.

Project management, at the highest and most efficient level, is like an assembly line. The raw materials necessary for the task are well-known and available, the machinery needed to combine the raw materials is in place and logically sequenced, the time necessary to combine materials is known and tracked, and the final product is produced in a predictable and consistent manner. The more effective the assembly line, the more consistent and predictable the output.

Coordinating has similarities, but is more nuanced. The high-level progression is the same (inputs—process—output), but the approach is different. Instead of an assembly line, think of coordinating like conducting a symphony orchestra. The raw materials are known—in this case, the sheet music is available. The musicians and the instruments are available, assembled, and capable of playing the music. Finally, there is the output in the form of a moving performance. The conductor has the latitude to influence the performance by evoking more emotion or tone from the musicians. The conductor can accommodate differences across venues and respond to the energy of the audience. An exceptional conductor does not see their role as enforcing strict adherence to playing the notes in the exact manner prescribed; they see their role as coordinating the efforts of the entire orchestra to ensure the most exceptional performance possible.

The best project managers direct and control the environment, removing variables and potential areas of non-conformity. By eliminating inconsistencies, they make processes more predictable and reliable. By contrast, exceptional leaders use coordinating to bring out the human dimension and the benefits it provides to others.

In this chapter, we will cover four dimensions of coordinating that exceptional leaders employ: collaboration, group and team dynamics, policy influence, and trust building. Exceptional leaders use these dimensions to coordinate others and elevate outcomes.

COLLABORATION

Over the years, we have had the opportunity to work with many fantastic leaders at all levels of experience. One of the most interesting trends that we have observed is that within leadership, the words we use can frequently be interpreted differently. Perhaps it is the complexity of language; per the Oxford English Dictionary, there are currently over 171,000 words in the English language. There are entire academic disciplines dedicated to language and the meaning of words. For example, linguistics is the study of language and pragmatics is the study of language in context.

We have found that words to describe leaders and leadership functions are commonly used interchangeably. As a living and continuously evolving concept, language can, and should, move in this way. However, it becomes challenging when terms like collaboration and coordination are so frequently thought of as identical. Take a moment and think about how you would differentiate collaboration from coordination.

What are the defining qualities for each? Where do the concepts overlap, and where are they distinct?

When you think critically about concepts like collaboration versus coordination, you establish self-awareness. Self-awareness helps you have the mindset necessary to develop and grow. If you don't have the appropriate mindset, you will not be able to apply what you learn effectively. Consequently, your journey to becoming an exceptional leader will be considerably hampered. You can improve your ability to learn, grow, and develop if you take the time to cultivate the right mindset in advance.

Now that you have a clear perspective on how you would define collaboration versus coordination, we would like to propose some common language. The dictionary definitions of the two terms are not very helpful in clarifying; collaboration is defined as, "to work jointly with others or together especially in an intellectual endeavor," whereas coordination is defined as, "the process of organizing people or groups so that they work together properly and well." Although the concepts are similar, we would suggest that collaboration is a fundamental component of coordination. For example, if you think of a basketball game, collaboration is what is happening on the court; coordination is what is happening in the arena. The players on the team are collaborating to achieve a common end and using the resources available to them to achieve that end. The arena is the venue for the collaboration; it is the reason there is a standard size floor with two basketball hoops, locker rooms, seating for fans, concessions, etc. Ultimately, collaboration is made possible through effective coordination.

Based on the common understanding that collaboration and coordination are not the same thing but are related, you should now have the mindset necessary to learn how exceptional leaders use collaboration to provide exceptional results.

Exceptional leaders demonstrate an ability to tap all the resources available to tackle an issue and lead others to a common end. Exceptional leaders are those who can make this process look deceptively simple. These individuals are willing to proactively go outside of their comfort zones and break down arbitrary silos to make sure they have access to all the necessary resources. There are physical resources that might be necessary, but leadership is about the resources inherent in others. Therefore, within a leadership context, the resources we are describing are the time, talents, and the attention of others.

To improve your ability to collaborate, we recommend three simple steps:

1. Approach issues and goals with humility.
2. Don't limit yourself to the resources that are immediately available.
3. Provide space for effective collaboration to occur.

When exceptional leaders approach an issue or work towards a goal, they do so with humility. Humility should not be confused with timidity or a lack of confidence. A confident and capable leader can still be humble. Humility is a safeguard against over-confidence. When leaders are over-confident, they limit their willingness to engage and collaborate with others. They might think they already know the answer or have the best way to address an issue. They are likely to overlook valuable assistance or insights. By contrast, collaboration is about bringing together all available resources.

Ask yourself if you already have a preconceived notion of how to proceed. If you do, take the time to think about alternatives — or, better yet, engage other resources to think about options. There may be opportunities for organic collaboration if you are willing to look for them.

Exceptional leaders are not limited by the resources that are immediately available. These leaders focus on what they need rather than what they have. They are willing to approach or source resources from totally different areas. For example, if you are leading a group that is very analytical, it might be helpful to collaborate with someone who is more artistic. If an artistic resource is not available within your group, you may need to look outside of the group for assistance. This might mean looking in a different part of the organization or maybe even to someone outside of the organization. We recommend you think about collaborations you have been involved with in the past. Was the group as effective as possible? Were there situations in which extra effort up front might have saved time and energy later? When you extend beyond what is immediately available to what is possible, you gain a broader diversity of perspectives and more effective collaborations.

Exceptional leaders provide space for collaboration to occur. As a leader, you need to be aware of the influence you might unintentionally exert when others are collaborating. We recommend taking on the role of facilitator rather than participant when it comes to collaboration. If you have engaged the right resources, one of the most important roles you can fill is to let those resources do the work. When you are overbearing or trying to control the process too much, you diminish the power of effective collaboration.

When exceptional leaders collaborate effectively, they access all the resources available to solve an issue or achieve a common goal. As you continue your journey to becoming an exceptional leader, we suggest you continue to think about how collaboration is such an important part of coordination and how coordination is such an important part of being a leader. If you can continue to develop your capacities, you will be able to lead more effectively and provide more value to others.

GROUP AND TEAM DYNAMICS

Think about all the groups or teams you have been involved with over the course of your lifetime. Professionally, you may be on a project team right now or serving on a committee board or running a lab. Personally, you might be in many more groups or teams: service groups, religious groups, special interest groups, or philanthropic organizations. In the past, you might have participated on sports teams, in bands, in youth organizations like 4-H, FFA, or the Boy and Girl Scouts. Regardless of which groups or teams you were involved with or when or how many, you have probably been on a group or team at some time during your life.

This is a good time to clarify what we mean by groups and teams. We chose to include both groups and teams in this section because the two words tend to have different meanings. The word "team" is usually associated with either sports or competition or professional work, whereas "group" is usually a less formal, all-encompassing term that can include more loosely affiliated collections of individuals—basically, a group or anything where people come together but don't call themselves a team. For practical purposes, we will use the dictionary definition of group: "A number of individuals assembled together or having some unifying relationship." We suggest that a group is limited in size, usually 3–20 individuals. A team is a specialized type of group; all teams are groups but not all groups are teams. For example, a basketball team would also be considered a group. However, a book club group would not necessarily be a team. For simplicity, we will address how exceptional leaders work with groups throughout the remainder of this section, with the understanding that any recommendations are applicable to teams as well.

Groups are everywhere, and they are becoming even more common where we work. There are trends towards self-directed groups in which the reporting hierarchy of command and control leadership is eliminated. Exceptional leaders embrace these trends and have the capacity necessary to address group dynamics.

There are three areas in group dynamics where exceptional leaders differentiate themselves. Exceptional leaders:

1. Are attentive to the group process, are aware of the stages of group growth, and draw out feedback from all group members.
2. Build better groups based on team members' strengths.
3. Recognize contributions of others by showing appreciation for individual excellence.

When individuals develop these capacities, they lead groups more effectively and are more effective at coordinating others. Let's go over them in more detail.

First, exceptional leaders are aware of the stages of group growth and draw out feedback from all group members. There are two interrelated concepts in this area: 1) exceptional leaders know there are predictable stages of growth associated with all groups, and 2) they make sure that all group members are engaged at each stage. These concepts are linked because awareness of the stages is necessary, but is meaningless if the group is not bought into the process.

One way to think about the relationship between these concepts is how a plant grows. The basic stages are seed, germination, sprout, plant, seed. However, if you put a box over the seed when you planted it, you would limit its ability to fulfill the other stages of growth. This is what it is like if you know the stages of group growth but do not make sure everyone on the group is engaged.

Probably the most well-known and validated model for group growth was developed by Bruce Tuckman. The stages he introduced included: forming, storming, norming, performing, and adjourning:

- *Forming* is when the group is first created, and no rules or norms have been established. During this stage, the leader needs to provide clear patterns and boundaries.
- Groups then move on to the *storming* stage. At this point, there may be conflict about how the group is run, or about what the expected outcomes should be. The leader cultivating positive conflict will help to clarify expectations and improve group alignment.
- The *norming* stage comes next. During this stage, the group members connect around the common outcomes decided on while storming. Leaders should work on cultivating and strengthening relationships among team members.
- *Performing* occurs when a group is established, focused, and connected. Leaders should work on making sure everyone continues to be engaged and maintains momentum.
- The final stage is *adjourning*. All things must come to an end. Some groups may be together for long periods of time, and some may only be together for a day or two. The adjourning stage is the recognized end for the necessity of the group. Referring to our plant example, this is when the flowers are pollinated, the fruit ripens, and the seeds for the next generation of plants are ready. Leaders should acknowledge this point to provide closure to everyone on the group.

Over time, and with practice, you should develop your own best practices for supporting groups moving through the five stages. All best practices, however, should involve all group members during each stage.

The second main area where exceptional leaders differ from other leaders is in the way that they build better groups based on group members' strengths. Groups are an interesting phenomenon, because they usually bring out the best or worst in people. Under poor conditions, groups are toxic and highly competitive. Under great conditions, groups are more productive, and everyone is more satisfied with the outcome than if the group members had worked independently.

We have seen the best and worst of group processes over the years. When teaching courses, we have always included a group project. Usually the assignment was to work with a philanthropic group, write a paper about the experience, and deliver a final presentation to the class. The groups would typically fall into two categories:

1. The groups that equally divided all the work amongst members, and everyone had some responsibility on the philanthropy, the writing, and the presenting portions.
2. The groups that looked at the entirety of the project and divided the work based on what made the most sense to the group members. Can you guess which groups tended to perform the best? Of course, it was the groups that divided the work based on what made sense to the group members.

Not everyone in the group is going to feel comfortable trying to set up a time with a philanthropic group. Similarly, not everyone is going to feel the most comfortable writing or presenting. Groups can be magical, because they provide individuals the opportunities to focus on what they are great at and passionate about. Exceptional leaders recognize how powerful groups can be and build better groups by focusing on group members' strengths. We are not implying that individuals should be pigeonholed; allowing individuals to focus on their strengths is empowering, not limiting.

One of the worst things educators can do is try to convince individuals that everyone should be great at everything. This is counterproductive to the educational process and who we are as individuals.

Everyone should have a basic level of competency across critical levels of education, math, writing, science, art, etc. However, when we try to be experts in everything, we inevitably become experts in nothing. Exceptional leaders appreciate what everyone can contribute and then coordinate appropriately to build on those strengths. Group dynamics are improved by this because members are more satisfied. When coordination is done properly, the total amount of effort required feels like less because everyone is contributing in the most appropriate way possible.

A final area where exceptional leaders excel in group dynamics is by recognizing the contributions of others by showing appreciation for individual excellence. There are a number of themes within this area that we want to draw your attention to. Specifically, exceptional leaders recognize contributions, show appreciation, and focus on individuals. One of the biggest mistakes we have seen leaders make when working with groups is to lose the identity of the individual members and begin to focus only on the group. The group is the vehicle for accomplishing something, but the group ceases to exist without its individual members. Exceptional leaders never lose sight of this fact and work very hard to make sure all members of the group feel appreciated and recognized as individuals in addition to the outcomes and accomplishments of the group.

Beyond individual recognition, exceptional leaders take the time to recognize the contributions of members and show appreciation. As humans, we have an innate desire to feel valued and valuable. Leaders taking the time to provide authentic appreciation, especially in groups, can be very powerful and rewarding for members. We recommend you think about groups that you have been involved with. Were members recognized for their contributions? If not, how would you have handled the situation differently? If recognition and appreciation were given, what are some situations where you think you might be able to use the same approach effectively?

As a leader, you are probably either involved with groups currently or will be at some point. If you can focus on developing these capacity areas now, you will be much more comfortable with group dynamics in the future. Remember that groups are composed of individuals; however, the power of the group is based in exceptional coordination that you as a leader can provide.

POLICY INFLUENCE

Exceptional leaders acknowledge the larger context in which their leadership occurs. Leadership is not in a vacuum; it is a set of responsibilities and actions interconnected with the much larger environment. Effective policy influence requires an immense amount of coordination on the part of a leader. An individual can make a difference and influence policy; however, influence is amplified exponentially when a leader can coordinate others in a mutually productive direction.

Exceptional leaders are those individuals who can see the forest for the trees. They are not so consumed with the tasks and administration associated with leading that they neglect to think about the bigger picture. Exceptional leaders do not need to be experts in influencing policy, but when they engage in policy discussions, their awareness, visibility, and perceived value increases tremendously.

There are generally two types of leaders: those who are at the mercy of fate and those who become the masters of their fates. Exceptional leaders know that failing to act is a failure of omission. Failing to become aware, involved, and failure to influence policy are failures to those you are leading. This may seem like a lofty expectation because it is. The world is in desperate need of exceptional leaders—individuals who recognize their responsibilities and are willing to act. When you seek to influence policy, you change the dynamic:

you are no longer at the mercy of fate; you are taking an active role in mastering your fate.

At a high level, policy influence includes five main steps:

1. Adopt a policy agenda.
2. Formulate the policy.
3. Adopt the policy.
4. Implement the policy.
5. Evaluate the policy.

One of the benefits of becoming more familiar and comfortable with this process is that you can apply it in many different situations. The intent of this section is to focus on policy influence, but you can use the above steps in many different influence settings.

The first step in the policy influence process is to develop a policy agenda. Simply, a policy agenda is what you'd like to accomplish. Take a moment to think about some law, regulation, or policy that influences you and that you would like to change. It can be something related to you professionally or personally, big or small. The key is to know what you want to accomplish and why.

After establishing a policy agenda, you need to formulate a policy. At this point, you need to help create the right level of support and political will to move the policy change forward. When formulating policy, exceptional leaders create different policy options to accomplish the same agenda. When policy makers have multiple options, it is easier for them to see how one particular option might fit their other motives. One way to think about this concept is the difference between fishing with a net and fishing with a single line and hook. With the net, you don't have to be as precise or lucky—and it's the same when you provide policy makers with multiple options. Why do you think there are so many additional provisions added on policy that cannot fail? It is the undeniably momentum of political will. This is where you want to locate your policy agenda.

Now think about the policy agenda you identified. How would you go about policy formulation? What options might result in your agenda?

Once the agenda has been properly formulated, it's time for policy adoption. During endless committee meetings and reviews, policy can start to lose touch with its original intent. It will be your responsibility to remain engaged in the process and to make sure this doesn't happen. There are several ways you might want to be involved in the policy adoption process, but we suggest that unless you are experienced with lobbying or influencing policy, you take a very simple approach. Specifically, make a commitment to yourself and find the time to follow the progress of the policy. You should be aware of important dates and milestones, and make every effort to be engaged in the process. Think about what additional support your policy influence might require to ensure adoption. If you proactively commit to the ongoing pursuit of the policy, you will be better prepared to take the time and energy necessary to follow through.

The fourth step is policy implementation. Once the policy has been adopted, implementation is the mechanism by which the rubber meets the road. Without funding or the ability to bridge the gap between expectation and reality, policy changes are intellectual exercises only. Exceptional leaders are aware of this reality and make sure that they help to identify and secure the means to get the policy implemented. They also assist to make sure any goals of the policy are translated into specific rules.

At this point in the process, we recommend you focus on making sure the policy is still consistent with the original goals. Even if certain concessions were necessary, which they probably were, if the intent of the influence is honored, you have been successful.

Recall the policy area that you would like to influence. Do you have a specific goal in mind? What are the alternate versions of that goal that you would be willing to accept? Any sort of policy is going to be modified and forced to evolve and conform throughout the implementation process. If you are not willing to demonstrate flexibility and coordinate accordingly, you drastically reduce the likelihood of success.

The final step in the process, and one that is frequently overlooked, is evaluating the policy. Evaluating means reviewing whether the goals of the original policy influence have been achieved. Exceptional leaders both support and participate in the policy evaluation process. The policy process can occur with the best of intentions, but sometimes the reality becomes distorted and inconsistent with the original intent. The evaluation process is meant to identify these inconsistencies and provide suggestions for resolving them. You do not need to be a formally trained evaluator to ensure policy evaluation occurs. Indeed, we recommend that you view your role as an ongoing policy advocate — someone who has a vested interest in making sure the policy is achieving the intended goals. If a policy has not been evaluated, we recommend that you coordinate with others to make sure evaluations are initiated. If evaluations are occurring, and their results show that the policy is not achieving its intended goal, we suggest you continue to try to influence the policy in the most beneficial direction.

The key is to stay engaged and involved. If you are willing to put forth the effort, you can make a difference and influence policy.

TRUST BUILDING

Trust is one of the bedrock necessities of exceptional leadership. It is a dynamic concept that links the perception of the leader's trustworthiness with the leader's ability to trust others.

When there is no trust or trustworthiness, all leadership interactions are in jeopardy.

Please take a moment to consider this statement. Trust is fundamental to exceptional leadership. With trust, there are many different leader errors or shortcomings that can be overlooked and forgiven. With trust, failures are understood in the right context and from the right perspective. Without trust, transgressions are blown out of proportion. Without trust, it is almost impossible to regain perspective or understanding. Exceptional leaders appreciate the importance of trust. They cultivate trust and are willing to make reasonable sacrifices to ensure they protect established trust.

Coordination requires trust. When you trust someone, and they trust you, it is much easier to work together. We don't always have the luxury of working with people that we like, but if we trust those with whom we are working, we should be able to tolerate them. If we don't trust someone, no matter how much we might want to like them, working with them over the long term is almost impossible.

Chances are you have either seen or participated in the infamous trust fall. In the past, the trust fall was one of the most common team building exercises. Generally, a volunteer would be placed with their back to the rest of the group and their arms crossed over their chest. The rest of the group assembled close behind the volunteer with arms outstretched, ready to catch them. The volunteer would fall backward into the waiting arms of the group. Although there are variations to the exercise, the overall message is the same: working with others requires trusting them.

What if, instead of being caught, the volunteer crashed right down to the floor? Do you think that individual would have difficulty trusting their coworkers again? Absolutely; for most reasonable people, falling to the floor when they expected to be caught would be traumatic.

Now think about a trust fall exercise in which the volunteer refuses to fall backward. The rest of the group might be ready, willing, and able to catch them, but all they end up doing is standing there waiting. What do you think the experience is like for the people waiting to catch the volunteer? They are probably bored and thinking what a waste of time the exercise is. Eventually, they may wonder why the volunteer is having such difficulty trusting them.

Although the trust fall exercise has become less popular over the years (due to the risk of physical harm and potential damage to team relations when things go wrong), it is still an appropriate example of why trust is so critical in leadership. Interestingly, both the volunteer and the group are applicable to leading others: the leader is like the group in that they need to be trustworthy, and is like the volunteer in that they need to trust others.

Exceptional leaders build trust in two primary ways:

1. They are willing to demonstrate their trust in others by coordinating with them.
2. They show that others can trust them by following through and being available.

The main point is that trust, in a leadership context, is a two-way street. Exceptional leaders know that it is not sufficient to trust others if others do not trust them. At the same time, it is not sufficient to have others trust them, if they don't trust others.

According to the dictionary, trust is "assured reliance on the character, ability, strength, or truth of someone or something." Think about all the people and things you put your trust in every day. You trust your alarm will go off in the morning; you trust the coffee maker to work; you trust your car to start and get you to work safely. The list of things that you put your trust in before you even start your day could fill a page. As humans, we have a natural inclination towards trust. Certainly, experience and biology affect our ability to trust and the level of trust we are comfortable with, but ultimately, we are naturally inclined to trust. Trust is why we don't have to spend all our time and energy growing the food we need to survive, because we trust that the food we can purchase is safe. Trust is fundamental and natural. As a leader, it is important that you embrace this perspective.

We once worked with an individual who had recently been placed in a leadership position. They had been a very strong individual contributor and so had been given additional responsibilities—asked to lead a team of three junior individuals. The transition was difficult for many reasons, but as we worked with the new leader, we found the main trouble came down to a lack of trust. This leader just couldn't trust that others were going to do the job as well as he expected. Consequently, he tried to take on too much of the work and ended up missing deadlines and running over on budgets.

We had this leader think about why he was struggling to trust others. He shared that it was the experience of terrible group projects while in school. Whenever there was a group project, he would inevitably end up doing all the work, because the other group members would not follow through. When he did trust others, their work was always lower quality than what he could have produced, so his grade would suffer.

Instead of having this leader think about all the things he had to trust before starting his day, we had him think about the things and people that he had to trust from start to finish. After 15 minutes of thought, he had come up with over 60 people and things that he put his trust in every day.

At this point, he had a revelation. The experiences of his past were undermining his current situation and limiting his future. He had no reason not to trust others in his current situation; they had not done anything to damage his trust in them. He freely gave trust to dozens of people and objects throughout the day without even thinking about it—yet when the stakes were highest, he was getting in his own way.

We recommend you go through a similar exercise. Think about how much you trust others and how that trust is affecting your ability to coordinate with them. If you don't have a high degree of trust, why not? Are there specific instances where your trust has been violated? If so, you need to decide whether the trust is repairable. If it is, you need to put forth the effort and time necessary to rebuild the trust. If you can't see how trust can ever be re-established, it might be time for a clean break. Too often, we obsess over no-win situations. We spend way too much time and energy trying to resolve that which can't be fixed. These are difficult decisions and should not be taken lightly; however, exceptional leaders know when it is time to move on.

If you are struggling to trust others but can't identify any instances where the trust has been violated, do some self-reflection on where the lack of trust is coming from. When you find having trouble trusting, we recommend you focus on the areas where you are naturally trusting and work to channel this natural trust into your leadership. You are much more likely to be successful in the long term if you can keep things simple and focus on what you can control.

The other trust-building area where exceptional leaders distinguish themselves from everyone else is trustworthiness. Unlike the ability to trust, which is impacted by previous experiences and natural dispositions, being trustworthy is something that you can immediately control. Trustworthiness is about being dependable and reliable, following through on your commitments, and being available. There is no special training required, no deep self-reflection, and no complicated process to follow. Being trustworthy is about consistently doing what you say. If you adhere to this simple principle, you will immediately gain trustworthiness.

Leaders get into trouble when they violate others' trust in them.

Perfection is unattainable, but exceptional leaders do their best to maintain the trust that has been placed in them. When leaders stumble and violate trust, it is much more damaging than when non-leaders commit the same violation. This is a burden of leadership. For example, when Lance Armstrong admitted to using performance-enhancing drugs, his trustworthiness was destroyed and his reputation may never recover. What he did is the same thing countless others do every day; however, most of these others live in obscurity, and so their violations do not carry the same penalties.

Think about how you conduct yourself as a leader. Do you deserve the trust that others place in you? If not, what do you need to change? Your trustworthiness is completely within your control; however, you must be willing to make the commitment and live up to this standard.

The journey to exceptional leadership is not an easy one. It requires faith and the understanding that all your efforts can be undermined if you are not vigilant about trusting others and being trustworthy yourself. Nevertheless, we are confident that you have what it takes to build trust as a leader right now. The more trust you can accumulate, the easier it will be for you to coordinate with others, and the more successful you will be as an exceptional leader.

SUMMARY

Coordinating is like the oil in an engine. Not the most glamorous aspect of the engine, but critical to its ongoing function.

Coordinating is not always appreciated until it is absent, but without it, leaders are not aware of their responsibilities to collaborate, address group and team dynamics, influence policy, and build trust. These dimensions are what elevate average leaders into exceptional leaders.

Just like an exceptional conductor can elevate the performance of an orchestra, an exceptional leader can elevate the performance of others through superior coordination. At the most basic level, a conductor must know how to read music, keep a beat, and point at people with a baton. If an individual were to develop these skills, they might be a satisfactory conductor, but they would never be exceptional. Being exceptional demands certain intangible qualities.

Many of the intangible qualities that we associate with exceptional leaders reside in their ability to coordinate. For example, exceptional leaders understand the value and importance of collaboration. They appreciate that collaboration is more than just mechanically bringing others together; it is the exponential value that you manifest when you bring people together and cultivate an appropriately collaborative environment. Exceptional leaders are attentive to group and team dynamics and continually monitor and adjust to changing conditions. They are involved with influencing policy and are not satisfied to be mere passengers. They use their ability to coordinate to have a much more substantial impact as a leader than they ever would as an individual. Finally, they continuously and relentlessly build trust. They are aware of the connection between and necessity for both trusting others and for being trustworthy themselves. They appreciate that this is the foundation of successful coordination as an exceptional leader.

Although a diverse set of topics resides under the coordinating header, it is one of the critical aspects of exceptional leadership. You may feel as though you are skilled in some areas and lacking in others. Exceptional leadership is a journey and one that will require significant effort and dedication on your part. However, if you are willing to put forth the effort and commit yourself to the end goal, you will become an exceptional leader.

PUTTING IT ALL TOGETHER

"Wherever you go, go with all your heart."

—*Confucius*

Our goal has been to provide you a comprehensive framework with which to develop your leadership capacity. We have frequently referred to becoming an exceptional leader as a journey, and we have done so on purpose. Exceptional leadership is not a destination; it is not an end state that, once achieved, stops the need for further action and effort. Too frequently, experts promote a vision of leadership that resembles that of enlightenment: a philosophical threshold that, once passed through, makes all clear. Too often, we are inspired by leadership development promises but then become discouraged when we don't see the results we were expecting. Sometimes, the results are performance-related—actual improvements in areas such as productivity or satisfaction. However, sometimes results are more internally directed—whether through improved insights, awareness, or authenticity. As humans, when we don't see the results of our efforts, we tend to lose interest and abandon the process.

As we conclude, we would strongly suggest that you take away three main points:

1. Your success on the journey to becoming an exceptional leader is directly related to the effort you commit and sustain.
2. Focus on simplicity in each area to begin with.
3. Don't become discouraged along the journey; results are accu-

mulated over time, not overnight.

Let's go over these in more detail.

First, as humans, any development requires effort. Think about a computer. You can install or delete software, clear the hard drive, or install a new operating system. The computer's memory is finite and multidirectional. This means a computer can have its memory erased without any trace of previous data retained. The addition and removal of data can occur until the physical limitations of the hardware are reached. By contrast, human minds are infinite and unidimensional. We cannot delete and unlearn what we have known previously; we can only accumulate knowledge. So many development programs fail because they do not recognize this simple underlying truth.

As a human, you have a vast store of accumulated experiences and knowledge. It would be foolish to think that you could unlearn all this experience and immediately implement the recommendations within this book. Much more productive approaches would be a) to acknowledge the importance and value of your previous experience, and b) to focus on how the recommendations in this book can complement your past or inform your future. This is how the effort you commit and sustain will ultimately determine your success on the journey to becoming an exceptional leader.

Reading this book is a commendable start; however, it is insufficient if you expect to see results. You must take the time to think about the recommendations, reflect on how they relate to your experiences, practice, and then reflect on the outcomes. This should be an ongoing process—one where you are continually refining and improving your manifest definition of exceptional leadership.

Second, focus on simplicity. Resist the urge to become mired in the details of the concepts we've covered. The simple fundamentals, the actions or capacities you can begin working on today, are those that will provide the largest possibility for improvement. As you continue to put forth effort, you will naturally begin to dig deeper and become more engaged in the details of the different areas. This is the expected progression, so don't worry about advanced details until you have fully mastered the simple concepts necessary to becoming an exceptional leader.

Third, maintain a positive outlook on your journey and don't become discouraged along the way. As you begin to put in the time and effort to develop yourself as a leader, you will likely notice the ways in which you are currently lacking. This is a natural outcome of becoming more self-aware. Suddenly, you can no longer live in ignorant bliss. The clouds have cleared, and you can see just how far it is to the top of the mountain.

This is the point at which you must have faith and the courage to continue. Everyone is familiar with the Chinese proverb, "A journey of a thousand miles begins with a single step"—and it is true. Becoming an exceptional leader is possible, but only if you are willing to begin.

We have never worked with someone who did not improve as a leader ... if they were willing to work at it.

As you continue along the journey, many of your improvements will occur in small and almost imperceptible ways. Think about the Grand Canyon; the Colorado River did not carve this geological wonder in a matter of days, months, years, or even decades. It took millions of years of the consistent and unrelenting flow of water. The results are abundantly visible today, but the ongoing changes are all but imperceptible.

Have the courage and faith to start today, and we are confident that you will become an exceptional leader.

ISSUE LEADERSHIP

At the beginning of the book, we provided leadership scholar Peter Northouse's definition of leadership: "Leadership is a process whereby an individual influences a group of individuals to achieve a common goal." We believe this is a fantastic definition, because not only is it simple, it also applies to many different leadership situations. It is just as applicable to someone volunteering to lead a youth program as it is to a CEO leading a large organization.

In the spirit of this definition, we would like to suggest our definition of an issue leader:

> *Issue leaders are individuals who use their relationships and character to strategically plan, act, change, communicate, support, and coordinate with others to achieve a common goal.*

The seven pillars of issue leadership differentiate our framework from other theories or models. We hope the practical and specific areas we have identified can serve as a guide for you and that this definition will provide a point of reference throughout your journey. When an individual masters the seven areas and learns how to use them appropriately, she will be exceptional as a leader.

NEXT STEPS

Now that you have completed this book, the next steps are up to you. As cliché as it is, the world desperately needs exceptional leaders. We have been fortunate enough to see the impact that leadership can have from Uganda to France to Chile to right here in our hometown of Athens, Georgia. There are no limitations to what exceptional leaders can accomplish. There is no maximum capacity for improvement or happiness or joy in the universe — there is only the need for exceptional leaders to unleash this potential.

Best wishes for a fulfilling and exciting journey. We can't wait to see what the future holds — and what you are capable of!

ACKNOWLEDGEMENTS

Although it is our names that appear on this work, it has been a monumental team effort to get here. Were it not for those that were directly, or indirectly, associated with this project it would have been impossible to reach this point. We are forever grateful to everyone that supported us throughout this process and shared their wisdom, suggestions, advice, or editorial pen. For those that we may have accidentally missed thanking on these pages, please know how much we appreciate your help on this journey.

First, thank you to our family. Our kids, Charlotte, Aiden, and Warren. You are the fuel for our purpose and the source of meaning for this work. We are amazed at the way you look at the world full of wonder and possibility. You inspire us, push us, and make us realize how blessed we are to be your parents, thank you. Thank you to our parents, Jean, Dennis, Valerie, and Ron. A lifetime of love, support, and belief in us is the bedrock for the ideas in these pages. To our siblings, Dana, Demian, and Chris, thank you for all your encouragement and patience.

Thanks to the team at Deeds Publishing in particular Jan and Bob, their guidance has been instrumental to moving from idea to finished product. Likewise, our friend and literary consultant Jeannie Ingraham has been equally fundamental to the process. Through endless calls and coaching sessions, she has been a beacon of stability.

Thank you to our friends and mentors that helped us refine and clarify our vision. In particular, Dr. Hannah Carter, Dr. Joyce Bono, Dr. Nick Place, Dr. Joe Joyce, and Dr. Grady Roberts. Thanks to our fellow colleagues and students at the University of Georgia and the University of Florida who both inspire and humble us with the amazing contributions you are making in the world each and every day.

Thank you to the experts that helped contribute to the ideas in this book. Collectively the experience and insights generated were nothing short of amazing. Thanks in particular to Beth Archer, Rob Black, Edmond Bonjour, Janelle Booth, Kim Coffee-Isaak, Lori Cope, Angie Cue, J.D. Dunbar, Lesley Fitzpatrick, Cindy Garretson-Weibel, Susan Harrison, Terry Hejny, Dan Hoffman, Marie Hvidsten, Steve Isaacs, Julia Latto, Mike Liepold, Jack Lindquist, Jim Mazurkiewicz, Monique McTiernan, Don Norton, Julian Pace, Monica Pastor, Vicki Pontz, Everett Rhodes, David Roseleip, Rochelle Sapp, Sarah Schlosser, Megan Seibel, Will Snell, Bobby Soileau, Michael Thomas, Larry Van De Valk, Rick Waitley, Joe Waldrum, and Laurie Wolinski.

Lastly, thanks to everyone that has served as a guide to us on our leadership journey. Whether by teachers, volunteers, work colleagues, 4-H, Accenture, Extension, Alpha Gamma Rho fraternity, professional organizations, or multitudes of other critical moments accumulated over a lifetime – your wisdom has left an indelible mark on us, and on the pages of the book. Thank you.

ABOUT THE AUTHORS

Drs. Kevan and Alexa Lamm are a husband and wife author team, who both serve on the faculty at the University of Georgia. They are parents of three amazing children and wrote this book thinking about the world their children will grow up in. Their purpose is providing others the tools they need to make a positive change in the world. Working with groups from Georgia to Uganda has given them the unique opportunity to see how one person can make a difference.

www.ingramcontent.com/pod-product-compliance
Lightning Source LLC
Chambersburg PA
CBHW030110100526
44591CB00009B/356